Let Prayer Change your Life

An Easy-to-Use, Exciting, and Fulfilling Approach to Developing a Prayer Life that Works

WORKBOOK

Books by Becky Tirabassi
from Thomas Nelson Publishers

Let Prayer Change Your Life (Revised)

*Transform an ordinary prayer life into one
that brings powerful results*

Let Prayer Change Your Life Workbook

*Analyze your prayer life and integrate a
daily appointment with God into your
schedule with this interactive guide*

My Partner Prayer Journal

*Develop a fresher, stronger, and more
exciting relationship with God with this
prayer organizer*

Quietimes Student Prayer Journal

*Help teens track prayers and answers to
prayers and build a solid, lifelong habit of
talking with God*

Let Prayer Change your Life

An Easy-to-Use, Exciting, and Fulfilling Approach to Developing a Prayer Life that Works

WORKBOOK

Becky Tirabassi

Publishers Since 1798

THOMAS NELSON PUBLISHERS®
Nashville

Published in Nashville, Tennessee, by Thomas Nelson, Inc.

Published in association with the literary agency of Alive Communications, P.O. Box 49068,
Colorado Springs, Colorado 80949.

Unless otherwise noted, Scripture quotations are from the HOLY BIBLE, NEW INTERNA-
TIONAL VERSION®. Copyright © 1973, 1978, 1984 by International Bible Society. Used by
permission of Zondervan Publishing House. All rights reserved.

Scripture quotations noted NKJV are from THE NEW KING JAMES VERSION. Copyright © 1979, 1980, 1982, Thomas Nelson, Inc., Publishers.

Scripture quotations noted TLB are from *The Living Bible*, copyright 1971 by Tyndale House
Publishers, Wheaton, IL. Used by permission.

ISBN 0-7852-7746-3

ISBN 0-7852-6658-5 (Revised)

Printed in the United States of America.

17 16 15 14 Victor Graphics 07 06 05 04

CONTENTS

Acknowledgments

Thanks to:
Vic, my publisher, friend, and adviser.
Carissa, my assistant, friend, organizer, and encourager.
Gina, my student writing colleague and friend.
Rog, my one and only husband, counselor, and best friend.
Jake, my one and only son.
And a special thank you to Thomas Nelson Publishers,
for giving me the opportunity to communicate about prayer!

I love you all,
Becky

GRASPING THE POWER OF PRAYER

I am convinced that prayer in a believer's life is an incredible, virtually untapped power source. Not only am I convinced because of my personal experiences, but the lives of many people who have been committed to the discipline of daily prayer, before and during our present day, validate that I am not alone in my discovery!

The following pages of this workbook, I pray, will serve as inspiration and motivation for you to grasp onto the power of prayer that is available through a scheduled appointment with God, making it an essential and integral part of every day. My hope is that you will be encouraged and exhorted to make a decision in your life to make prayer a priority.

Upon recognition that prayerlessness was sin in my life,

I was deeply touched by God to make a commitment to pray for one hour a day. Over 16 years (and many "hours") later, God has changed my personality and character, increased my faith through unbelievable answers to prayer, called me to accountability in numerous areas, and given me a vivid vision of possibilities for His will in my life. Having been a teenage alcoholic, I know that this disciplined prayer life is a work of the Holy Spirit within me, not a performance that I have proudly perfected.

The unfolding of the discipline of prayer in my life was an unexpected surprise. I'm not the kind of person you would typically find sitting still for one hour, much less quietly praying all that time. But because of prayer, these years of daily time with God have resulted in an incredible journey with Christ.

In 1984 I attended a Youth For Christ (YFC) convention where many speakers spoke convincingly about prayer. Had I known that each convention keynoter would concentrate on the subject of prayer, I might not have gone. At that time, prayer was not a big interest to me as a Christian. I wanted to see conversions and be considered dynamic. But because of the speakers' personal convictions and God's Holy Spirit, I made a decision in February of 1984 to pray for one hour a day for the rest of my life!

Though that may sound pious or even spiritual, it was neither. I had a deep, unmet desire to know God better and to love Him like I had when I first met Him.

Within weeks of this new discipline in prayer, my whole life and my limited perspective of God changed. He was no longer too small, too strict, or too far away. He was near, present, and always with me. I recognized and acknowledged His power, His creation of me and the world around me.

Prayer showed me a whole new way of living. Is it time for you to go to the school of prayer? Is it time for you to cling to God on a daily basis, hear Him speak, obey His will, and let Him change your character through prayer?

The principles that you will be challenged to try and test in this workbook have been tried and tested by thousands of others. They have led to mounds of miracles and numerous opened doors, and will lead you in a deeper walk with God as well.

I urge you to release God's power through a new (or renewed) practice of prayer in your life. If, in fact, you are content with your fellowship with the Lord on a daily, perhaps hourly, basis, I trust this time will be refreshing. But if you turn to this workbook out of a deep hunger for effective, powerful prayer, be open to God's Holy Spirit and believe that your life will never be the same because prayer does, prayer can, and prayer *will* change your life.

PART ONE

THE DISCOVERY OF PRAYER

VICTORY OVER PRAYERLESSNESS BEGINS WITH HELPLESSNESS

I always enjoyed a convention to get out of a spiritual lull. Speakers, singing, challenge. Hmmm. Yes, if there ever was a time in my life when I needed a lift or renewal, it was now! Before leaving Cleveland for the fortieth anniversary of Youth For Christ convention in Chicago, I had come to the conclusion that this spiritual drought was the result of burnout—overwork, little rest, and too much responsibility. Therefore, I had purposed in my mind to quit the ministry. It seemed an appropriate time to leave the working world, relax, omit outside stress, and just be happy *inside*.

But the first speaker at the convention shocked me with

his comment: "If you think it's time to quit, it's too soon!" This had happened to me before. Through a person, God was speaking to me. As if I were the only person in the room, the words from that one sentence resounded and echoed in my ears until I acknowledged that they were directly from God—to me.

God seemed to be saying, "Don't get up. Don't go anywhere. Don't daydream or pretend you don't hear My voice. You've been looking for answers, and I'm going to give them to you . . . though not what you might expect."

Sandwiched between perfect strangers, I didn't dare move. Without a friend to verbalize this experience to, I sat back, exhaled, then took the slow, deep breath of a person curious with anticipation. Though somewhat afraid of what God might say or do, I nervously awaited something unusual or supernatural to occur.

Then it unfolded, on cue, but without rehearsal. Each keynote speaker had been asked to speak on how God had been at work in the Youth For Christ organization over the previous forty years. Though none of them were given a more specific theme, there was one unexpected thread—especially for my ears—prayer.

Prayer? If the convention had been promoted as a prayer conference, I would have never considered attending it. Not that I didn't believe in prayer and its value for the Christian. I just had not, up to that point in time, considered prayer instrumental in my daily walk with Christ. Oh, I "prayed." I kept a journal of written conversations with the Lord. When in distress or trouble, I regularly released an "I need HELP" prayer. I often found myself asking God for a parking space close to a store entrance during a rain- or snowstorm, but sadly, that was the extent of prayer in my Christian life.

Certainly, young, busy Christians shouldn't be expected to carry on with such a serious (and boring) discipline, should they? Prayer, to be perfectly honest, was not a priority— though it was a principle I believed in and encouraged others to do the same.

Like a bombshell, it hit with the second speaker.

Even as he began to share, his sincerity about God, ministry, and prayer became evident. He told of regular, daily intercession for the salvation of his neighbors. I was struck with the thought of his incredibly busy schedule and amazed that he made time to pray for his neighbors. I didn't even know my neighbors' names!

As he continued, his tone of voice rose, and his intensity flared as he pounded out the words of James 4:2. Looking at those of us who needed to call on God's power most and probably used it least, he cried, "You do not have because you do not ask! James 4:2." I actually opened my Bible to the verse thinking that it couldn't really say that—at least, not in that way. It wasn't that blatant, was it? Then he choked up with tears and proceeded to impress upon the listeners the fervency of his message: "Prayerlessness, for the believer, is sin."

How he phrased it, said it, or convinced me, I'm still unsure, but the Holy Spirit began His own conviction on Saturday morning I cried in silent shame and humiliation through every general session because of my lack of prayer, as each godly speaker related tremendous miracles of healing, incredible circumstances of God's intervention (for example, opening the doors of India to the gospel and YFC after a twenty-four-hour prayer vigil), and even the harvest of souls saved years later *due to daily, consistent prayer.*

Their stories magnified and illuminated the self-sufficient approach to ministry and daily Christian life that I was living because of the sin of prayerlessness. By then, only one word aptly described my state: *ashamed.* I was ashamed of myself for the audacity to lead Bible studies, evangelize, work for God daily, but spend no personal time with Him in prayer, in conversation, or even in confession.

As the weekend came to a close, we were invited to choose from a list of various optional seminars. Like a neon light flashing on the pamphlet was a workshop on prayer. That would be my choice.

As my good friend and I were standing at the entrance to this workshop, laughter seemed appropriate to break up the serious mood of my desire to want to go into a workshop on prayer. Both of us had the feeling that the discipline of prayer was an extremely serious matter, but neither of us did anything that was that serious (at least up to that point in time).

Parting ways, I slowly entered the workshop feeling awkward and hesitant. I picked a seat in the back of the auditorium with the thought that I could still leave the room if it got too serious or boring.

Once again, tears flowed down my cheeks uncontrollably throughout the hour presentation on prayer as the speaker talked of the power available to a believer who prays. To make matters worse, no one else in the room seemed to react to the speaker with similar emotion, and my blubbering appeared out of place. I just couldn't pinpoint the root of all of this!

But God's work was being completed within me. Through the weekend and culminating with this workshop, I was indeed convinced that prayerlessness in the life of this believer was sin. If I truly believed that spending time with God in prayer was actually engaging in conversation with my Creator, Friend, Savior, Leader, and King, why would I overlook, avoid, forget, or fall asleep in the middle of prayers? If I truly wanted to be used by God to evangelize and disciple the world for Christ, why would I place so little emphasis on time alone with Him?

My perspective on prayer was changing.

I sat frozen as all three hundred workshop attendees filed out of the room. I was probably an interesting sight with streaked makeup and red puffy cheeks. I just didn't want to leave the room without making dramatic changes in my life, but where to start and how to maintain them seemed beyond my grasp.

Then a woman touched my shoulder, offering to pray with me, about . . .

I bowed my head, determined to make a lifelong decision to . . . to . . . to . . . change, I guess. Change what? Change how?

Then words of prayer flowed from my mouth with the same intensity and mystery as my initial prayer for salvation had come so desperately from within me seven years earlier. Without premeditation, I made a decision in front of God and another person to pray for an hour a day for the rest of my life!

I knew myself too well. If I had given God a trial period to see if "I liked it" or if "it fit into my busy life," I would have allowed the decision to pray an hour a day to fizzle into a sweet memory as a "too difficult for me" discipline.

No, I sensed God's presence and provision in this decision, and I had been weighing the benefits of prayer in a believer's life versus life without it all week long. It was a hands-down decision to pursue the discipline.

Mentally drifting back to the seminar, I remembered a number of verses and principles about prayer the speaker had explained. Not a single verse had been new—Matthew 6:31–34; 7:7–8; and Philippians 4:6–7, 19—yet for the first time, those words were alive and fresh and inviting. Their practicality pierced me as I mentally walked with them through a typical day. As I toyed with actually believing them, they stunned me with their power.

An hour a day. I had to take a radical step closer to God. I took the plunge and left that room bathed afresh in the power of the Holy Spirit. It was all I could do to find Kinney, my friend, go to lunch, and pour out to her all that I felt God was saying to me. Something was coming alive within me. The relationship with God I had experienced as a young "on fire," baby Christian was aglow. That dependency, that willingness to be guided by God, to listen to Him, to share every thought with Him, was reignited within me as acceptable, not as childish. With the true style of an evangelist, I elaborated on all that I had heard and all I was certain that God was going to do in my life because of prayer. We laughed, we cried, and both of us thought how special this convention had been—certain God had touched our lives.

It was to be beyond my wildest expectations what power God would release into my life from that day forward because of prayer, but first, I had to master the discipline.

O. Hallesby, author of *Prayer*, profoundly submits that

"nothing so furthers our prayer life as the feeling of our own helplessness." This admission—or concession—offers great hope to those of us who might be discouraged in our self-effort and continuous lack of victory in the pursuit of a true and fulfilling prayer life.

Andrew Murray in his classic *The Prayer Life* discusses prayerlessness in the life of a believer, even and especially the minister, at great length. He concludes, "If we recognize, in the first place, that a right relationship with the Lord Jesus Christ, above all else, *includes prayer*, according to God's will, then we have something which gives us the right to rejoice in Him and to rest in Him" (emphasis added).

Could prayerlessness be sin in your life? Is it a concept you might even consider? Comment.

_____

_____

_____

_____

_____

_____

_____

SIGNS OF PRAYERLESSNESS

Before, during, and after my six-year stint with alcoholism, I had the opportunity to take the type of survey that asks you if you have any of the signs or symptoms that lead to or denote alcoholism. Depending on how honest I was being with myself, or how desperate I had become, I always found myself saying yes to some or most of the questions. The intention of that simple quiz was to cut quickly to the heart of the matter: There is a problem.

Early in my discovery of prayer, I was interested to find that O. Hallesby had designed a similar questionnaire for people potentially struggling with prayerlessness. It seemed paradoxical that such an issue could be considered as dangerous as alcoholism. But when prayerlessness is placed in the context of one's whole life and relationships, O. Hallesby considered it a great stealer of one's relationship with God and others, a threat to the ability to ward off sin, and a sign of laziness after God. Would you like to take the test?

List of dangerous results of prayerlessness:
- ☐ We have more "world" in our thoughts.
- ☐ We feel farther away from God.
- ☐ We have less "God" talk in our conversations with others.
- ☐ Slowly an unwilling or rebellious spirit creeps into our personality.
- ☐ Sin doesn't sting as much, because it is less honestly confessed.
- ☐ We deal with sin as the world does, by hiding it!

The purpose of taking this test and coming face-to-face with prayerlessness is not to humiliate or discourage you, but to allow you to surrender yourself helpless in achieving victory over prayerlessness on your own. (If you've been in a Twelve-Step group, this concept probably sounds familiar.)

If prayer is not a priority in your life, why not? What is?

_____

_____

_____

_____

_____

_____

_____

Prayer might not be a priority in your life for a variety of reasons. Pinpointing the main reason will be helpful in overcoming the defeat that you have been experiencing in wanting to spend regular time in prayer. Your reasons might include the following:

- Your life reflects laziness toward God. (Samuel Chadwick said, "The crying sin of the church is its laziness after God.")
- You are bored in your spiritual life.
- You are weighed down by sin.
- You have not been convinced of the power in prayer.
- You have many misconceptions about prayer.

I had been a Christian for almost eight years when I truly discovered prayer. At the time, I was under thirty, most of my friends and coworkers were my age, and all of us were relatively young Christians—most of us coming to Christ as high school students or as young adults. Our frame of reference regarding prayer was liturgical, dramatic conversion-type experiences, or we saw it as a means of opening and closing meetings.

Because we were peers teaching peers, we had very few role models in the spiritual discipline of prayer. And the lack of models led to many misconceptions about prayer, surely adding to our lethargy and excuses regarding prayer in our lives.

Take this misconception survey, ranking yourself from 1 to 10 (1 being never, 10 being always). The purpose of the survey is not to give you a score or rating but to help you identify any misconceptions you hold. Even *one* misconception can keep you from praying.

Misconception #1: Prayer is boring.

1	2	3	4	5	6	7	8	9	10

Misconception #2: Prayer is only for the pastor or a prayer warrior.

1	2	3	4	5	6	7	8	9	10

Misconception #3: God doesn't always answer prayer.

1	2	3	4	5	6	7	8	9	10

Misconception #4: My prayer has no power.

1	2	3	4	5	6	7	8	9	10

Misconception #5: Prayer is for older people.

1	2	3	4	5	6	7	8	9	10

Misconception #6: Doing something else is more productive than praying.

1   2   3   4   5   6   7   8   9   10

Misconception #7: God knows everything anyway, so why pray?

1   2   3   4   5   6   7   8   9   10

Misconception #8: I'm so busy; He'll understand.

1   2   3   4   5   6   7   8   9   10

My admission of helplessness, the realization that I held many misconceptions about prayer, and an agreement with God concerning my neglect of prayer gave me the impetus to move away from prayerlessness and become a daily, consistent, effective, and powerful pray-er.

If it is time in your life to pray a prayer of confession, admitting your prayerlessness and/or any other sin that you could be cherishing in your life that has kept you from God, begin with an honest prayer in the space provided.

_____

_____

_____

_____

_____

_____

_____

_____

_____

From numerous books on the power and potential available to a believer who prays, I found quotes that were often simple but went straight to my heart. For instance, O. Hallesby expressed what I could not articulate but was feeling: "Neglect prayer. Neglect God." Or the words of Peter Marshall: "The whole field of prayer, and praying as laying hold of unlimited power, is unexplored, with the result that spiritual laws still lie undiscovered by the average believer. Sometimes in our desperation, we hit upon the right way to pray, and things happen—our prayers are gloriously answered. But for the most part, our praying is very haphazard and the results are often disappointing." Haven't you felt that way? Doesn't it make you want to shout, "You, too?" These authors, with their insights into prayer, gave me hope that I might be able to master prayer.

Having once been helpless to overcome prayerlessness, then experiencing a change in my perspective of prayer, I am compelled to share my discovery with others! As I closed the first chapter in *Let Prayer Change Your Life*, I would like to close this chapter with C. S. Lewis's words to be challenged to change with "a fellow-patient in the same hospital who, having been admitted a little earlier, could give some advice."

CHAPTER 2

CHALLENGED TO CHANGE

How would you like to have a thermometer in your relationship with God that measures closeness, fondness, loyalty, and desire to be with Him? When we experience a continual desire to know God better, it resembles any other vibrant, healthy relationship—we look forward to being together! But avoiding, fearing, sidestepping, and averting conversations with the King in prayer can be red flags, signaling trouble ahead or need for adjustment.

Have you experienced any noticeable difference in your intensity level in your relationship with God in the last few months or even the past year? Explain what you think that might be about.

_____

_____

_____

_____

_____

_____

_____

When you think about spending time in prayer, how do you feel?

☐ Excited
☐ Indifferent
☐ Obligated
☐ Numb
☐ Full of dread

Take the next few minutes to check your faith thermometer, based on the characteristics listed below. Rank yourself on a scale of 1 to 10 (1 being below freezing, 10 being sizzling hot). When you're finished, you'll know in which areas you can improve.

Integrity quotient *(I am honest and ethical in my relationships and/or my business dealings.)*

1   2   3   4   5   6   7   8   9   10

Focus and determination *(My priorities are in order: God, family, work.)*

1   2   3   4   5   6   7   8   9   10

Knowledge of your gifts and call in life *(I know what my spiritual gifts are, and I am using them based on this season of my life.)*

1   2   3   4   5   6   7   8   9   10

Humor, patience, and hope levels *(I am not easily angered; I look to encourage; I wait patiently.)*

1   2   3   4   5   6   7   8   9   10

Joy in serving the Lord *(I am enthusiastic to share my faith and gifts with others.)*

1   2   3   4   5   6   7   8   9   10

Expectation that God desires to answer your prayer *(My belief in God's ability to answer my prayers is firm and strong.)*

1   2   3   4   5   6   7   8   9   10

Witness to healing and miracles of spiritual, physical, or emotional nature *(I am experiencing and/or I am part of a small group or support group that is witnessing God's healing touch in our lives.)*

1   2   3   4   5   6   7   8   9   10

Hunger for the Word of God *(I read the Word daily. I look forward to hearing God speak to me.)*

1   2   3   4   5   6   7   8   9   10

Openness to prayer with others on the spot *(I offer to pray with people, not only pray for people.)*

1   2   3   4   5   6   7   8   9   10

Quick acknowledgment that God is responsible for something in your day and/or life *(I have eliminated the words luck, chance, and coincidence from my vocabulary and realize God orchestrates the details of my life.)*

1   2   3   4   5   6   7   8   9   10

Here are a few more questions:

Do you remember an experience with God that included great forgiveness, His intervention, or an especially awesome moment of recognizing His power or sensing His presence in your life? Refresh your memory of that day, moment, or event by detailing the experience in the space provided.

_____
_____
_____
_____
_____
_____
_____
_____
_____

If you desire to carry on a two-way conversation with God, you must position yourself to hear His voice. A daily, regular Bible reading plan will allow you the optimum results.

Do you carry a Bible with you in your car, briefcase, or purse, or do you have one in your office desk to easily access, research, and use at any time in any day? Why or why not? Explain.

_____

_____

_____

_____

_____

_____

How have you regularly read the Bible in the past (for example, going through the *Change Your Life Daily*™ *Bible*, reading a chapter a day from the beginning of the Old Testament to the end of the New Testament, or using other devotionals)? List your methods in the space provided, and after listing, number them in their order of effectiveness in your life.

_____

_____

_____

_____

_____

_____

_____

PRAYER ATTITUDE

Sometimes when a group or individuals promote my prayer workshop to their congregations or communities, they are met with common responses, such as:

"Are we going to have to pray for three hours?"
"Isn't this just for the women of the church?"
"I'm awful busy."
"Oh, that's a place for the prayer warrior, not for me!"

When you are invited to a prayer meeting, what is your initial response? Do you look forward to and plan to attend prayer meetings? Do you have to force yourself to attend? Do you make excuses? If so, why do you think you do?

_____
_____
_____
_____

Would you consider prayer a priority in your life at this time? Explain.

_____
_____
_____
_____

When you hear of answers to prayer, how does that make you feel?
☐ Motivated to pray
☐ Discouraged about my prayer life
☐ Skeptical
☐ Other: _____

On a scale of 1 to 10, rate the significance of prayer in your life (1 being insignificant, 10 being extremely significant).

1   2   3   4   5   6   7   8   9   10

After answering these questions, you might be feeling a bit discouraged or overwhelmed. Instead, make note of any negative attitudes or misconceptions you might have about prayer, and press on. Date this first series of questions, and answer them again in a month to see how much you've changed.

PRAYER ACTION

Prayer is a time commitment. If we consider it something to do later on in the day—or even in life—we will procrastinate forever.

Has there been constant nagging, tugging, or pulling on your heart to spend time with God? Describe any circumstances, sermons, incidents, books, or Scriptures that you have been drawn to that might be God's calling you to consider prayer a priority in your daily life.

_____

_____

_____

_____

_____

_____

_____

_____

PRAYER APPLICATION

Prayer becomes a priority only after it becomes a non-negotiable part of your life. Consider *other* areas in your life where you have been both successful and unsuccessful at achieving consistency or discipline.

Successful at . . .	Unsuccessful at . . .

What appears to make the difference in your ability to achieve success? Is it the good it brings to you? Is it the pay? Or the rewards? How do you *feel* about the areas where you have achieved success?

_____

_____

_____

_____

_____

_____

As for the areas where you have not achieved success, is there a level of compromise? Have you been willing to schedule the time you need in order to succeed in this area? Can you identify a reason that you are forgetful, negligent, or resistant to this?

_____

_____

_____

_____

_____

_____

THE SECRET OF MY SUCCESS

When it came to the discipline of prayer, I found one key that led to success for me. It was not evaluating, considering, or weighing the amount of discipline it would take to achieve a daily time with God, but it was *deciding to make an appointment with God* and put it on my calendar that worked! Those initial appointments have led to the consistency, success, and uninterrupted pattern of one hour a day since February, 1984.

When your level of desire to make a change grows in an area, the first obvious or outer change will be in the way you spend your time. A decision to make time for something new will be an outward reflection of your inward commitment. For instance, regularly lifting weights will lead to noticeable, increased muscle tone and definition. But with prayer, you will notice more than outward physical changes. The supernatural aspect of God's presence and provision in your life will become evident to everyone around you!

In my experience, just *wanting* to pray wasn't powerful enough to *get* me to pray. Being aware of my lack of prayer and feeling remorse over my laziness in prayer were positive motivators in drawing me closer to making prayer a priority, but they still were not enough. My dilemma was emotional, physical, and spiritual. When I understood that I was ignoring God and hurting myself by ignoring God, I was ready to make the time commitment to pray.

Believe it or not, after all the agonizing over where and how I would find more time in my already busy day to pray, all I had to give up was a little sleep and a little television viewing.

Complete the following: The things I would have to give up in order to pray each day are

_____

_____

_____

_____

_____.

By making a new, daily commitment to spending time with God, I was acknowledging that I had been living life fairly independent of Him. More than anything, I wanted to return to a dependency on God as I had experienced as a young Christian. In becoming dependent on God as a new believer, I had to give up control of things and habits. In deciding as an older Christian to make God a priority in my life, I had to give Him control over my time.

PART TWO

FROM DECISION TO DISCIPLINE

CHAPTER 3

KNEE DEEP
IN DISCIPLINE

Concentration while in conversation with the King came when I wrote my prayers. Written prayer was

a record of my words to God.

a record of His responses to me.

a way to stay focused.

a key to avoiding distractions and daydreaming.

an accountability tool.

a method of making my appointment more like a real meeting.

an organized way to spend my hour in prayer.

a systematic way to remember to pray for people I told I would pray for them.

proof that God answered prayer.

eye contact, reminding me that this was a two-way conversation.

a record of my life, my walk, my journey on earth.

GOD CALLING

After making my "prayer" decision at that 1984 Youth For Christ seminar, I began to assess and evaluate the circumstances, Scriptures, and sensitivity in my spirit to prayer. I was amazed at my audacity to make such a commitment to pray one hour a day in front of another person. Because that decision was unlike anything I would have come up with for myself, I grew convinced that God Himself was calling me to this adventure in prayer. And God is calling others!

Many times people will come up to me at a prayer workshop and say, "I've been asking God to teach me to pray, and this method is just what I need. It's an answer to prayer!" Or they will say, "I believe I was supposed to be here today to make this commitment in prayer," or "God has been calling me to spend time in daily prayer, and I'm not going to run any longer." When we finally believe that God is calling us to pray, an extra measure of confidence is released to make an unusual commitment in prayer.

When I look back, I am so glad that I allowed many of the pieces that had fallen together over the previous few weeks and days to convince me that I was going to be able to do this. After only two days, I concluded that those keynote speeches, radio shows, Scripture references, and Spirit-led promptings were meant to give me courage to overlook my past failures with daily prayer and just do it! Ultimately, they provided motivation I needed to be where I am many years later . . . praying one hour a day.

Do you identify with the feeling of being "led" or "called" by God to prayer? Summarize the feelings or circumstances you've experienced that lead you to believe this. If you haven't felt a desire to pray, use this space to write a prayer, asking God for His direction and leading in your prayer life.

_____

_____

_____

_____

_____

_____

_____

_____

IMMEDIATE RESULTS

If you have never previously spent regular time with God, but will make a decision to do that, I guarantee you will experience immediate results. An initial change might begin with your vocabulary—everything from swear words to slang words or phrases just might disappear! I also had a new conviction about luck. After I had specifically prayed about something, then watched it come to pass, I found I no longer felt comfortable saying, "I was lucky." *Luck* and *chance* left my vocabulary for good. My new response to an answer to prayer was a quick "Thank You, Lord" under my breath or in my mind, or sometimes I responded with a genuine eruption of "Praise the Lord!"

Other physical and outward changes occurred in my first week of prayer. I began to look much more carefully at how and where I spent my time. I found a new discipline to work out and exercise regularly. But this time, I did not give my workouts more time on a weekly basis than prayer, which had been the case before I began to pray an hour a day. I easily quit watching certain TV shows (such as soap operas), and I no longer felt comfortable going to certain movies. Whether they were good or bad, I couldn't seem to justify spending time that way. I had not even asked God to change those areas in me. And though I was not expecting an increased desire for purity and integrity to be the result of my daily prayers, it occurred.

Are there some rough edges around your daily life (language, habits, or laziness) that you would be excited to see God turn into an increased desire for purity and integrity? List them in the space provided.

_____

_____

_____

_____

_____

_____

I was also surprised by how much I enjoyed spending time with God and getting to know Him better. I had feelings of love toward Him developing in me. Consequently, the result of these new—or renewed—feelings caused me to act according to the way I felt toward God. I found it much more painful to hurt, embarrass, or shame Him as a greater love for God and a new inner strength grew within me.

Even as I uncovered personality flaws about myself during prayer, God's love seemed to form a strong wall of protection around me, helping me face up to and fight against the sin in my life. The inevitable moments where God encouraged correction in my life were buffeted by a soft blanket of His comfort and concern surrounding me, making the discussions bearable.

How often do you feel God's love? (Check one.)
- ☐ All the time
- ☐ Off and on throughout the day
- ☐ Once in a while
- ☐ Rarely
- ☐ Never

THE POWER OF PRAYER

Soon, I was rediscovering the power of prayer! For me as an adventurous person, the power of God through prayer had initially drawn me to Him. As a baby Christian, I saw God change many difficult circumstances, heal my addiction, and take my life in a completely different direction because of prayer. By reestablishing a regular prayer life, I was seeing God's power released again. I often wonder how I could have so easily forgotten the power of prayer.

Andrew Murray and a group of South African ministers in the early 1900s determined that the lack of power in the church at that time was due to a lack of prayer. They called prayerlessness a deep-rooted problem with the ministers of their denomination. They concluded that a lack of prayer in their lives resulted in a lack of spiritual power in their denomination and in their country. I assessed that the reentry of prayer was a power booster to every facet of my life. C. S. Lewis in *The Screwtape Letters* presented prayer as a weapon of the believer that the enemy wants to undermine and make useless because it is so powerful. Could this be a description of your perception and/or practice of prayer?

Do you feel a lack of power in your Christian life? List the ways you feel or have felt powerless.

_____

_____

_____

_____

_____

_____

Andrew Murray articulated in hundreds of ways and in many books that "prayer is in every deed the pulse of spiritual life." Not only did Andrew Murray influence me with his writings about the state of prayer in the church and in an individual, but Leonard Ravenhill's profound assertion about a person's practice of prayer nailed me as well: "No man is greater than his prayer life."

Check the adjective that best applies to you. My prayer life today is

☐ great; I'm really connecting with God!
☐ good, but not exciting!
☐ okay, but could be better!
☐ not so good and really needs help!

Knowing how limited my knowledge of prayer was, I began to devour any books that I could find on the topic. Many were old, yellowed paperbacks, tattered and forgotten on various office shelves or on the sales rack in Christian bookstores. I found the words of Peter Marshall, Ros Rinker, George Mueller, Leonard Ravenhill, and Andrew Murray describing

- where I had been in my prayerless Christian walk.
- the unknown territory I was heading into with my new decision to pray.
- what I could expect to find when I got there:
  ☐ Power
  ☐ Direction
  ☐ Miracles
  ☐ Brokenness
  ☐ Favor
  ☐ Healing and hope

From the preceding list, check the item that is the most desirable today for your life.

I discovered for myself that prayer was meant to be powerful, give direction, release miracles, bring healing, and offer hope—and because of the excitement in that message, I was compelled to share my findings with others. The most awesome result of my discovery was that I believed that these powerful principles and patterns in prayer were not just for the Andrew Murrays and George Muellers—they were for me and for you. However, they had to be tapped into and practiced.

CHAPTER 4

PRIORITIES, PERSPECTIVES, PERSONALITY, AND POSSIBILITIES

The excitement and adventure of prayer in my life included a shake-up of my priorities, a shift in my perspective of God and prayer, a personality overhaul, and new and exciting possibilities for the future. With the good came the hard!

A SHAKE-UP

First, I realized I wouldn't be successful in the discipline of prayer if I just looked for time with God. I had to *make time* with God. When I came to the conclusion that I needed to and wanted to spend time with God, I faced the reality that my *priorities* would have to change.

What will have to change for prayer to become a priority in your life? List the habits or hobbies that you might have to give up, limit, or reschedule to establish a regular time with God in your week. (For example, the cost I paid to pray one hour a day was a little less sleep in the morning and a little less television viewing in the late evening.)

_____

_____

_____

_____

_____

_____

Andrew Murray wanted so much for people to understand that intimacy with God takes place when we pray. He said, "God needs time with us. If we would only give Him time." By making time for God in our daily lives, we are inviting Him to influence, encourage, empower, and speak to us. When we neglect time with God, we have to ask ourselves, What has become so important that it is more important than God? Am I overcommitted in any one area rather than balanced physically, emotionally, socially, and spiritually? Could I intentionally be avoiding God's counsel or advice?

Answer these questions as honestly as possible in the space provided.

Review your week as you are currently spending time. First, insert your time commitments and appointments into the weekly schedule on page 38. Then, pencil into the semi-full schedule fifteen- or thirty-minute daily appointments with the King that you would be willing to keep.

Peter Marshall fondly referred to prayer as the place where you get your "marching orders from the Captain!" After spending time in prayer, your whole day seems to fall into place. During conversations with the Lord, you will find the reason and ability to say no more (and without guilt) and yes when and because you have heard God call, confirm, or send you.

Leonard Ravenhill said, "Those who prayed most, accomplished most." When I first read that quote, my type A personality struggled with the concept. How could sitting still produce and accomplish more than activity? My basic misconception about prayer was that I equated it with sitting still. Once I discovered the action of prayer, I found it to be the place where ideas, to do's, and action steps were birthed.

If you talk through your plans and projects with God— before performing them or attacking them head-on—clarity of conviction and direction will result in forward progress toward your goals. Efficient, wise, and divine planning is a

	SUN	MON	TUES	WED	THURS	FRI	SAT
6 AM							
7 AM							
8 AM							
9 AM							
10 AM							
11 AM							
12 PM							
1 PM							
2 PM							
3 PM							
4 PM							
5 PM							
6 PM							
7 PM							
8 PM							
9 PM							
10 PM							
11 PM							

FROM DECISION TO DISCIPLINE

direct result of prayer. You'll observe for yourself that the more you pray, the more productive you become.

Do you believe that God wants to direct every step of your life?

☐ Yes   ☐ No   ☐ Not sure

On a scale of 1 to 10, how willing are you at this time to ask Him to direct your life (1 being very unwilling, 10 being very willing)?

1   2   3   4   5   6   7   8   9   10

A SHIFT

The next change that I experienced because of daily prayer was that my *perspective* of God and prayer was redefined. I saw prayer as the place to ask God for advice: "What would You have me to do? Where would You have me to go today?"

As a practical application, have a two-way conversation with God that resembles the previous example. Write down any thoughts that come to your mind after you ask Him those direct questions. To picture the situation, put yourself in a quiet place, and record the words you say and the thoughts that occur. Include any Scriptures that come to your mind.

_____

_____

_____

_____
_____
_____
_____
_____
_____
_____
_____
_____
_____

The purpose of that exercise was to help you establish and desire

- two-way conversation with God.
- dependence on God.
- genuine curiosity about His will for you.
- comfort in both talking and listening to God.
- practice in prayer.

Did you struggle in any way with this concept of having a two-way conversation with God? Explain.

_____
_____
_____
_____
_____
_____

Were these words easy to express in writing? Explain.

_____

_____

_____

_____

_____

_____

After praying for one hour every day, my perspective of prayer changed.

I learned that prayer is not a monologue to a deaf God, but a conversation with a God who hears prayer.

Prayer is not helping God with an answer; it is asking God to help. It is not telling God what to do; it is telling Him my needs. It isn't so much for the disciplined as for the undisciplined!

Prayer is not necessarily meant to be an easy joy ride, but it definitely is a spiritual discipline that produces joy.

Prayer is not just coming to Jesus; it is letting Jesus come into me.

Prayer is not only for the educated seminary scholar; it is for anyone who will practice, persevere, and plan to pray.

Prayer is not a substitute for time in the Word; it will lead _to_ the Word.

Prayer is not for the impatient but for the one who waits.

Prayer is not a place to boast but a place to confess. Prayer is not my motivating God, but God's motivating me.

Prayer is not a waste of time; it is an appointment with the King of kings.

At this time, what is your definition of prayer?

_____

_____

_____

_____

_____

_____

_____

AN OVERHAUL

Next, a *personality change* began to occur. At first I was taken by surprise when personality flaws came to the surface. The truth is, I wasn't really surprised, but embarrassed (or afraid) to face those areas in my life that I had been avoiding. I recognized unforgiveness, bitterness, and resentment. Formerly, I considered each a bad habit; now I called them sin.

I want to encourage you, as this happens, not to be afraid or to resist their emergence. Eventually and ultimately, the confession and turning from sin will lead to healing and growth.

How comfortable are you with admitting your weaknesses and shortcomings to others?

_____

_____

_____

_____

_____

How about to God?

_____

_____

_____

_____

List some of your fears as you think about confessing your sins to God and/or others.

_____

_____

_____

_____

The impact and impression that God's Word and presence will have on your life when you spend time with Him daily often result in (1) a change of attitude, and (2) a turn from negative or stubborn habits, such as procrastination, unforgiveness, and anger. In prayer, you can't hide those destructive (and sinful) ways from Him—or yourself—any longer. During a time of prayer, you will gain courage to make lifestyle adjustments, as well as the ideas, thoughts, and creative (though sometimes humbling) suggestions on how to walk away from your old ways, old nature, and maybe even old friends and hangouts.

Without thinking long or hard, can you think of any old ways or bad habits, any unforgiveness toward someone who has hurt you, or resentment or jealousy in your life that you and

God would probably talk about if given the time, freedom, or permission?

_____

_____

_____

_____

_____

_____

I reread *Let Prayer Change Your Life* in order to write this workbook. On page 49, I share about the struggle in my life (previous to writing *Let Prayer Change Your Life* in 1990) of not being able to give cheerfully. A few years later, I read the story as if I never was that person. Over time and apparently with God's strong influence in my life, I find giving one of the most fun opportunities I have as a Christian. I give my regular gifts cheerfully, and I truly enjoy giving big or special gifts. It is a confirmation to me that not only will one's personality change, but it will change in noticeable, visible, unusual ways—even to the extreme opposite of one's previous way of behaving.

In the space provided, discuss one struggle or area in your life that you would like to see changed by God.

_____

_____

_____

_____

_____

As your priorities and personality change, and a refreshing, renewed perspective of God and prayer begins to take hold in your life, your purpose for life truly comes into focus. I believe what God had planned all along for us becomes clearer and clearer through prayer. We begin to live with certainty and enthusiasm, power and faith, and an abiding hope as the impetus behind our steps. Then we experience the fulfillment of our dreams and goals.

EXCITING POSSIBILITIES

The next exciting change dealt with the many possibilities I had for living out my adventurous, renewed faith. Prayer became the place where I viewed God as the architect or designer of my life plan. It is where I discussed with Him and where He revealed to me my life's blueprints in a manageable work schedule that promised to unfold in the proper time. Two-way conversations with God became the juncture where God delivered His possibilities for me in the form of ideas, opportunities, forgotten dreams, and former goals. They come flooding into my mind no longer as impossibilities but as possibilities.

What might these possibilities look like in your life? Will they be reachable? Robert Schuller, a former pastor of mine, challenges believers to consider God a willing giver, not a reluctant withholder. He said two things I have never forgotten and I always refer to when I am in the midst of a project:

"When God gives you an idea, it won't go away," and "You don't have a money problem; you have an idea problem."

These two statements remind me that if this is God's idea for me, He will provide the ways and finances to fulfill it. They remind me that I am not alone in having to achieve, fund, or make this happen. God *will* help me. And so, I find myself often asking God for an idea!

What has been a dream in your life that has yet to come to pass? Explain.

_____

_____

_____

_____

_____

Take time today to ask God for an idea to help you reach this dream. Record any thoughts that come to mind during prayer.

_____

_____

_____

_____

_____

_____

_____

_____

Most people don't believe me when I tell them that I am not inherently organized. They see my travel schedule, writing schedule, and production of videos and think I must be very organized. I'm truly not an organized person by nature, but I believe that my appointments with God have contained conversations that allow me to define my goals and develop action steps to turn them into accomplishments. I have learned to *act on* the thoughts, ideas, and possibilities that come to my mind and out on my paper during prayer. After many years, the process continues to work the same way for me.

Ideas that are thoughts during prayer build momentum over time, giving me confidence to take them from my mind and put them onto paper or speak them out loud to someone else. From there, a God-confidence increases my faith to make phone calls, write letters, enlist others' prayers, and pursue the action steps that seem appropriate. Soon, I begin to see doors open or close.

In addition, I've come to understand that a closed door doesn't necessarily mean no. I might need to be persistent, knock on another or a new door, reevaluate my direction, put the brakes on to wait for better timing, or just be patient (ah, yes, patience).

Prayer will affect not only *one hour* of your day but *every hour* in your day!

CHAPTER 5

HOW TO PRAY THE "WRITE" WAY

When I was a preschooler, a Sunday school teacher told our class that the word *nowhere* describes God. She told us that we can look at God as being "no where" or we can picture Him as being "now here." Same word. Same spelling. Different perspective.

What is your perspective on God's presence in your daily life? Describe it in the space provided.

_____

_____

_____

_____

_____

The perspective of prayer that is most helpful in drawing me daily back to an appointment with God is to picture Him as "now here"! A threefold pattern unfolds as I invite Him to talk with me:

1. I *prepare* my heart for prayer.
2. I *plan* time for prayer.
3. I *practice* the art of prayer.

Let's discuss each part, and you can give it a try.

1. PREPARE YOUR HEART FOR PRAYER

First, close your eyes and picture yourself with the Lord. Are you walking with Him? Are you in a favorite place? Are you at the beach or fishing? Are you by a fireplace in a soft chair or in a garden? Take some time to think about this . . . the where and when. Personalize the setting. Make it yours to return to at any given moment. Expect God to be with you there. Consider Him present, not distant.

Describe in writing what you experienced.

_____

_____

_____

_____

_____

_____

_____

_____

_____

_____

_____

_____

_____

_____

_____

_____

_____

_____

Describe your meeting place.

_____

_____

_____

_____

_____

_____

_____

_____

_____

_____

_____

_____

_____

Having an attitude of expectation may initially seem foreign to you, but meditate on Psalm 5:3: "In the morning, O LORD, . . . I lay my requests before you / and wait in expectation."

Are you comfortable waiting for the Lord in expectation? Explain.

_____

_____

_____

_____

_____

_____

_____

Each day, begin your prayer time by quieting yourself or closing your eyes. This approach will prepare your heart to both talk to and listen to God.

2. PLAN YOUR START

If you fail to plan, you plan to fail (W. Clement Stone).

In developing a quality quiet time with God, being comfortable and relaxed is very important. Be practical enough to know

- *when* would be an ideal uninterrupted time for your appointment with the King.
- *where* might be the very best place for you to pray. (Note: What works well for some might not work at all for you!)

Most people suggest that the best time to spend with God is early in the morning. But if you are not an early riser, when would be the best time for you? If you have unscheduled afternoon or evening time that you can carve out of your day, you are fortunate. But if there is no other uninterrupted part of your day, then the next obvious adjustment you need to make is either (1) to go to bed earlier or (2) to set your alarm earlier than usual. If you are disciplined or serious enough to make prayer a daily priority, but haven't been able to schedule the appointment with the King into your calendar, try one of these time slots:

- Immediately when you get home from work or school *before* returning calls, etc.
- At lunchtime, whether you work in an office, go to school, or are at home

- After the kids are fed and put down for naps or bedtime
- When you otherwise might watch a particular television show
- After driving kids to a practice and just staying in the car to wait for them (instead of running errands)
- While you commute to work on a bus or train or in a car (using headphones with praise music playing loud enough to drown out other noises)
- After driving car pool, but *before* the day's chores begin
- Right before getting into bed at the day's end

When do you think might be a good time for you to meet with God? (Choose one from the list, or consider your own.)

_____

_____

_____

_____

_____

_____

I have found that every day is different in my life. I am most effective at time management when I look at my calendar from a week-at-a-glance perspective. After observing each day while looking over the entire week's travel, family, and appointment schedule, I pencil in my seven days of appointments with the King. This method has been the most effective and realistic way for me to spend a full hour each day with God, and it allows for the fewest changes or adjustments.

Even choosing a special place to pray has been an important part of my success. Ideally, the room or chair or desk I choose should provide a peaceful atmosphere, be a quiet place, and offer freedom from interruption. (Be warned: Don't sabotage yourself by choosing a good time of day, but the wrong place.)

Does a specific place come to mind that might be a good one for your prayer time?

During the week?

_____

_____

_____

_____

On weekends?

_____

_____

_____

_____

Whenever there are other people or appliances in the near vicinity (such as children, teenagers, seatmates, stereos, or television), you will be distracted. So plan your time and place for prayer around others' schedules as well. For instance, if you are an at-home parent, instead of using the first part of a child's nap time for doing chores, use it for your quiet time. Allow doing chores or making phone calls to float over into time when your children are otherwise occupied with their friends or favorite television shows or videos, or when they can help you with the chores.

Consider using your commuting time for prayer rather than spending that hour in random conversation or in magazine or newspaper consumption. *But* bring along a personal cassette player with a variety of instrumental music, drowning out competing noises. This causes others to ignore you, sensing you are preoccupied or busy.

The key is to plan. Plan ahead. Plan wisely. Plan for interruptions, but plan.

3. PRACTICE YOUR PART

Practicing—or rather, developing—the discipline of prayer works like any other sport or habit you would like to become better at or more comfortable with. It will take

time and effort,

review and evaluation, and

continued education.

Not long after I made the decision to pray for one hour a day, I found myself wanting to become an excellent pray-er. I am competitive by nature, and though I never took my athletic skills to a level higher than AAU competition, I saw this prayer discipline as something I could focus on and excel in if I chose to put forth the effort.

Written prayer was critical in lengthening my attention span during prayer as well as personalizing my conversations with God. Writing (or journalizing) became my tool to focus on God during conversations with Him. It allowed me to concentrate and have direction rather than count on my memory to get me through a prayer list. In addition, written prayer provided accountability and served as a deterrent to daydreaming. Having paper and pencil available—and in extra supply—afforded a measure of consistency and held off those sneaky, weak reasons not to pray.

Have you ever kept a journal of your daily thoughts or happenings, or have you ever written your prayers? Describe your experience. (Was it positive, negative, exciting, boring, etc.?)

_____

_____

_____

_____

_____

_____

_____

_____

_____

_____

_____

_____

_____

_____

_____

_____

_____

_____

PART THREE

THE DESIGN FOR PRAYER

CHAPTER 6

ONE CHRISTIAN'S SECRET TO A HAPPY HOUR

I'm not inherently disciplined. Are you? Actually, very few people I know can master any discipline easily. Most personalities have some level of procrastination and a greater love for fun than love for hard work. Therefore, for me to master the discipline of prayer, I had to resort to something that was easy for me. The transformation from prayer as a part of my lifestyle rather than a dreaded discipline occurred when I placed my hour of prayer onto my calendar and into my current method of scheduling meetings and making appointments.

The appointment idea allowed me to be as nonnegotiable with my time commitment to prayer as I would be with any other meeting on my calendar—especially if it was with

Someone who was
  royal,
    famous,
      intelligent,
        advisory,
          special,
            loving,
              unconditional,
                powerful, or
                  wise!

Appointments or meetings with special people are rarely—if ever—canceled, overlooked, pushed back, or forgotten. In fact, they are planned for, anticipated, and carefully scheduled so as not to be rushed, abruptly ended, or mishandled in any way. Literally writing the initials *QT* into an hour block on my daily calendar led to the ultimate success of having never missed or forgotten one of my hour appointments with the King in more than eleven years.

Praying for the sake of fulfilling a duty as a "good" Christian is much less motivating than picturing myself in a quiet spot talking to Jesus. By writing my prayers, I made eye contact and remained focused in my hour appointment with the Lord, which was often missing when I just closed my eyes and tried to pray.

My original purpose for written prayer was to overcome these weaknesses:

- Daydreaming
- Worrying about pressing tasks (instead of praying)

- Being distracted enough by a ringing telephone to answer it instead of ignoring it and continuing to pray

In chapter 6 of *Let Prayer Change Your Life*, I shared that the actual idea for *My Partner Prayer Notebook* (now titled *My Partner Prayer Journal*) came during a prayer. In my prayer, I simply asked God for an idea. I honestly expressed to Him my desire to keep accountable and get organized in my prayer life. Because my daily life was already organized by calendars, notebook dividers, and to-do lists, I believe God used a method that was familiar and was working to show me how I could both organize and become successful in my prayer life.

WHAT HAPPENS WHEN YOU PRAY?

When I decided to define prayer in my own words and determine what actually happened when I prayed, I could identify two actions: (1) God talked to me, and (2) I talked to Him. Prayer was

    a two-way conversation

        that could take place

            at any given moment

                between anyone and God.

Prayer was expressing myself honestly to God, and it included listening to Him. Looking at prayer from this perspective caused me to conclude that my prayer time needed "my part" in prayer and "God's part" in prayer.

Have you ever thought of prayer as a conversation with God?
☐ Yes   ☐ Sometimes   ☐ No

If not, why not?

_____

_____

_____

_____

_____

If so, do you spend as much time talking to as listening to God? Explain.

_____

_____

_____

_____

_____

My Partner became the affectionate title and name for my prayer notebook. My P.A.R.T. in prayer followed this pattern:

P—for PRAISE prayers
A—for ADMIT prayers
R—for REQUEST prayers
T—for THANK-YOU prayers

And God's PART in my prayer notebook was designated by these letters:

L —for LISTENING to God and not talking

M—for MESSAGES, where I recorded sermon notes, etc.

N —for NEW TESTAMENT

O —for OLD TESTAMENT

P —for verses in PROVERBS that either convicted me or comforted me

I even included a housekeeping or miscellaneous section in *My Partner Prayer Journal* called "TO DO." This TO DO section proved to be a place to write down thoughts, ideas, chores, phone calls, and projects that came to mind during my hour in prayer. The purpose of this section was to make note of what I was to do later that day or week without forgetting to do it or having to do it right at that moment.

CHAPTER 7

MY PARTNER PRAYER JOURNAL: MY P.A.R.T

L ord will you just show me what to do?"

My Partner Prayer Journal was the answer to that very prayer! I asked God to help me get organized and keep accountable to my hour of—and in—prayer. During that prayer, the details of *My Partner Prayer Journal* unfolded.

Develop a quiet time notebook and call it *My Partner*. Divide the journal into two parts:

1. My P.A.R.T.—where I talked to God and believed that He was hearing every word.

2. God's PART—where He talked to me and I listened to His every word.

Through this planned pattern of two-way prayer, I found that my prayer life contained every important facet of communicating with God.

My P.A.R.T. in prayer had four sections where I journaled prayers of PRAISE, ADMISSION, REQUEST, and THANKS.

God's PART of *My Partner Prayer Journal* included the sections in which I recorded what I felt God was speaking to me during times of LISTENING and not talking; after hearing sermons or MESSAGES; while reading the NEW TESTAMENT and OLD TESTAMENT and PROVERBS as regular, planned Bible reading; then noting any TO DO's that came to mind while I was praying.

By dividing my journal into types or sections of prayers and providing blank lined paper in each section, I soon became organized in my approach to prayer, yet sill spontaneous and free-flowing within each section.

For example, I found that because I had a designated ADMIT section, I was prompted to confess my sins on a daily basis rather than conveniently forget that part of my prayer life (as I had done so many times before). And by writing out and having a visible, tangible prayer list in a REQUESTS section, I became very consistent and specific in intercession for others.

Have you ever struggled with confessing your sins daily or with remembering to pray for people who where in need of it? (Check one.)

☐ Never   ☐ Rarely   ☐ Often   ☐ Always

Explain.

_____

_____

_____

_____

The discipline of writing my prayers also provided a new sense of accountability in my thoughts and words, commitments and decisions, requests and confessions. I was less casual in approaching God, yet daily I grew more confident that He was listening and responding to me with a consistency that I had never before experienced. By recording my daily conversations with the Lord, I could literally see when prayer was being answered. This practice was strong enough to overcome the disappointment that came with haphazard praying.

By including daily planned Bible reading and meditative, quiet moments at the last part of my hour in prayer, I allowed God's voice to become the answers or responses to my prayers.

Describe the prayer routine that you have practiced (prior to reading _Let Prayer Change Your Life_ or _Let Prayer Change Your Life Workbook_).

_____

_____

_____

_____

_____

What solutions, if any, does an organized system for prayer bring to your previous prayer problems?

_____

_____

_____

_____

_____

_____

_____

_____

My Partner Prayer Journal has been my Bible's daily companion since 1984, enriching my appointments with the King and bringing accountability and organization into my prayer life. *My Partner Prayer Journal* can be ordered through My Partner Ministries (see the last page of this book for information) or purchased at a Christian bookstore. If you are feeling creative or highly motivated, you might enjoy making a personalized prayer journal. But if you truly want to begin writing your prayers and are procrastinating simply because you have to *make* a prayer journal, take the next step and get a copy of *My Partner Prayer Journal.*

PRAISE

The PRAISE section of *My Partner Prayer Journal* is the beginning point in my conversation with God. I see (or picture) Him joining me—wherever I am— to have a two-way conversation. Though I believe He is always with me, at this time I most sense His presence or feel Him sitting down with me one-on-one.

When I try to imagine what it will be like to actually see the Lord face-to-face for the first time, I expect that I will be compelled to tell Him how wonderful I think He is—or PRAISE Him! I can see myself telling Him how good and kind He is or how powerful and faithful He has been toward me and my family.

The PRAISE section, by design, is where I focus on God, not me. It is the place where I convey a

*P*urposeful
*R*everence and
*A*we of God's
*I*ntegrity and
*S*overeignty
*E*ternally!

Fill in the blanks with five adjectives that positively describe God in your own words.
Lord, You are _____, _____,
_____, _____, and
_____.

To be honest with you, if I were to sit down to pray without a plan, I believe that I would end up filling my hour mostly with requests and perhaps even a bit of daydreaming. Therefore, the PRAISE section has become a commitment or decision of mine to spend time every day telling the King of kings, the only One who deserves praise on this earth and in heaven, how much He means to me!

How often do you offer praise to God in your daily life? (Check one.)
- ☐ All the time
- ☐ Off and on, throughout my day
- ☐ Every once in a while
- ☐ Only when I'm in a church service or prayer meeting
- ☐ Rarely, if ever

Over the years, I have found that praising the Lord is as much an attitude as it is an action. One of the best ways that I have found to personalize my praise prayers is to rewrite and paraphrase the Psalms. In fact, I have read and paraphrased two to ten psalms in numerical order every day for the past eleven years.

As I rewrite the Psalms, I believe that I am

- learning how to praise God by following the written prayer examples of the Psalms.
- agreeing with the psalmists in echoing their praises to the Lord!

By my praying through the Psalms, my heart has grown after and in love with God. It is truly the time and place in my daily prayer hour that I can say and feel the words, "I love You, Lord."

When was the most recent time that you told the Lord you truly loved Him? Share your experience.

Because this PRAISE section is also the beginning of my time in prayer, I usually date the first page and note the time that I am starting to pray.

Example:
DATE—March 12, 1994, at 7:15 A.M.
Psalm 146: Praise the Lord, O my soul. I will praise You, O Lord, as long as I live, with all of my life. I will not put my trust in princes or in men who cannot save. But You, the God of Jacob, remain faithful forever. You uphold the cause of the oppressed. You give sight to the blind. You lift up those bowed down. You love the righteous. You reign forever.

Now, you try it. In the space provided, try these various exercises designed to encourage you to express your praises to God. Even if it seems awkward or difficult at first, remember you don't need to conjure up feelings for God or pretend that you feel a certain way about Him. The key to experiencing an authentic time of heartfelt praise toward God is expressing your true, honest, and sincere feelings about Him to Him—exactly where you are at this very moment and on this very day in your life.

If you are

      wounded in spirit or emotion,

            failing in an area of your life, or

                  discouraged with a specific situation,

this should not hinder you from praising God. You'll be comforted to know that many of the psalmists' prayers arise from their insecurities as well as from their confidence in God. So praise God in the words that genuinely reflect your relationship with Him today and always.

Personal Praise #1

Rewrite any portion of Psalm 34, putting into your own words any of the verses that express how you feel about God today.

_____

_____

_____

_____

_____

_____

_____

_____

_____

_____

_____

_____

_____

_____

_____

_____

_____

_____

_____

_____

_____

_____

_____

_____

_____

_____

_____

_____

_____

_____

_____

Personal Praise #2

In addition to—or instead of—praying the Psalms, you might consider yourself a poet, songwriter, or painter expressing your praises to God in your own special way. Let your creativity flow—and remember you'll never be judged or critiqued for your style, punctuation, or spelling! In the space provided, write or create your praise.

_____

_____

_____

_____

_____

_____

_____

_____

_____

_____

_____

_____

_____

_____

Personal Praise #3

Any lyrics, choruses, or hymns that are familiar or favorites of yours are perfect examples of how to personalize praise prayers in this section of your time with God. You can write out the words or sing the melodies as your praises flow from your heart in admiration for the Lord.

_____

_____

_____

_____

_____

_____

_____

_____

_____

_____

_____

_____

_____

_____

_____

_____

_____

_____

_____

_____

_____

_____

_____

_____

_____

_____

_____

_____

_____

Because of the PRAISE section of *My Partner Prayer Journal*, I have become convinced that God's love is unfailing. I have read through the Psalms (and seen through my own life) that He desires to protect us, nurture us, be faithful to us, and even discipline us because He loves us! When my lips "overflow with praise," those praises come from a person who knows and has experienced God's love on a daily basis. They are not the words of an observer who notices how God loves others and works in their lives. No, these are my personal praise prayers, and they will become yours as well.

ADMIT

Search me, O God, and know my heart;
    test me and know my anxious thoughts.
See if there is any offensive way in me,
    and lead me in the way everlasting (Ps. 139:23–24).

The words in these verses have provided the consistent pattern in which I begin the ADMIT section of my prayer time. As I write out these verses, I give God entrance and permission to illuminate the sin, failures, temptations, and shortcomings in my life.

Almost every day, I have written—in longhand—the words of Psalm 139:23–24 at the very beginning of my admit prayer. These words seem to get to the point and show me the heart of where I am in my relationships with God and others.

Just the practice of saying to God, "Search me," is inviting Him into my deepest concerns, thoughts, doubts, fears, and failures. When I pray, "Know my heart," I'm acknowledging that He knows me better than anyone. Then asking Him to "test my anxious thoughts" and to "see if there is any offensive way in me" allows Him to correct, comfort, counsel, and forgive me.

The "search me" prayer prompts me to agree with God about how I have been acting and even divulge the secrets and resentments that I might be hiding or holding onto. It is my way of telling the Lord that I am willing to talk with Him about these issues. By asking Him to "lead me in the way everlasting," I am saying that I want to do His will, walk in His ways, and avoid the ways that perpetuate denial, destruction, and death.

How significant is admission or confession in your prayer life? (Check one.)

- ☐ A very important part
- ☐ A fairly significant part
- ☐ A small part
- ☐ No part at all

To be a clean vessel, to have a clear conscience, and to give the devil no foothold in my life, I believe it is a must to confess my sins to the Lord on a daily basis. I see this discipline as the key to having and maintaining right relationships with God and others. I consider daily admission or confession of sin to be nonnegotiable, especially if I desire to be an effective and powerful pray-er (Pss. 66:18; 84:11; James 5:16), which I do! And last, but not least, I am convinced that a willingness to daily confess my shortcomings, and request God's searchlight to expose these areas to me, is a definitive step toward being the most godly person, parent, spouse, friend, and co-worker that I can be!

Though it is uncomfortable for most of us to admit that we have

> fallen short,
>> hurt another,
>>> lost our way,
>>>> been selfish,
>>>>> manipulated,
>>>>>> harbored hatred or resentment,
>>>>>>> cheated,
>>>>>>>> stolen from or
>>>>>>>>> lied to another,

confession needs to be part of every believer's prayer life. The ADMIT section is not meant to be comfortable; *it is meant to produce a change of heart and direction.* Admission provides an opportunity for us to be cleansed, renewed, and transformed on a daily basis.

Is admitting your mistakes or faults to yourself uncomfortable for you?

☐ Yes   ☐ No   ☐ I don't know.

Is admitting your mistakes or faults to others uncomfortable for you?

☐ Yes ☐ No ☐ I don't know.

Is admitting your mistakes or faults to God uncomfortable for you?

☐ Yes ☐ No ☐ I don't know.

Why or why not?

_____

_____

_____

_____

_____

_____

_____

_____

My First Confession

When we first enter into a personal relationship with Christ, one of the first things we admit to God is that we have "sinned and fallen short." Many of us at the time of conversion, or at a point of asking Him to be Lord in our lives, told God specifically what we were sorry for, how we had sinned, and whom we had hurt, and we admitted that we had hurt Him as well (Rom. 3:23). The Bible assures us that God responds to those initial confessions—and every subsequent confession—in this way: "If we confess our sins, He is faithful and just to forgive us our sins and to cleanse us from all unrighteousness" (1 John 1:9 NKJV).

In the space provided, describe your experience with confession, if any, at your time of conversion.

_____

_____

_____

_____

_____

_____

_____

_____

_____

_____

Especially because I publicly share my testimony two or three times a month, I am often reminded of the day that I became a Christian. The janitor (not the pastor) of a church led me to Christ in a very simple prayer in the church's basement. This occurred at a time when I was completely without help for my addictions and without hope to make it another day. By the way, this little conversion ceremony was not a spectacular, well-attended event. But the janitor had his theology right. He invited me to repeat the sinner's prayer after him, asking me to say the words out loud:

Dear Jesus, I am a sinner. I need You, and I am so sorry for what I have done to hurt You and others. [He gave me the opportunity to confess in detail any sins that I could name or remember . . . and I did, though it took a while.] Please forgive me and change me. Come into my heart, and fill me up to overflowing with an extra measure of Your Holy Spirit. Lord, I need You. I love You.

Before I prayed the prayer with Ralph the janitor, he told me that the Bible said when a person invites Jesus to come into her heart and life, and asks Him to forgive her for her sins (2 Cor. 5:17), she becomes brand-new—and the old person passes away! Though this sounded too good to be true, I hadn't a better offer, so I went ahead and prayed the prayer.

Upon praying the sinner's prayer, I can honestly say I had an experience with God. I can look back and recall the remorse, humiliation, and self-hate I had before I prayed the prayer. And undeniably, after I confessed my sins in front of God and another person, I absolutely felt released from the heaviness of shame and guilt, forgiven, and clean, not dirty. The experience of confessing *all* of my sins—immorality, alcoholism, and drug addiction (just to name the biggies)—in front of another person had an obvious effect on me. Within days of that prayer, my lifestyle radically changed (James 5:16), and I experienced many healings: emotionally, spiritually, and physically.

In the basement of that church, I experienced the supernatural principle of forgiveness. I confessed my sin; I told God that I hated it and would turn from it, and I said I needed His help to get out of my addictions. My response after experiencing this unexplainable and undeserved love and mercy was to turn from the drugs, alcohol, and immorality as fast as I could run from them.

Have you ever experienced the power of forgiveness as described above? If so, describe the feelings you experienced. If not, write a prayer asking God to show you His power in this area, or explain why you feel you haven't experienced this.

_____

_____

_____

_____

_____

_____

_____

_____

_____

_____

_____

_____

Had someone lined up all of the people that I hurt, betrayed, lied to, or cheated on, they certainly would not have allowed me to feel free from the guilt or shame for my offenses. In fact, they might have hoped that I would pay them back, make up for my wrongs, or do "penance" to make right my wrongs.

But not God. He forgave me, the sinner that I was, not because I had paid the price or even promised to change. He paid the price. His death on the cross canceled the debt of my sin. His willingness to forgive me became an inward sign of how much God loved me. The knowledge of God's unusual love for me, a sinner, caused me to walk away from my old life. I felt forgiven for my past and loved, even though I had been so far from God, and I was given an opportunity to change into a new person.

My Daily Confession

To this day, I do not know the name or address of the church where I prayed the sinner's prayer—or even the janitor's last name or his whereabouts. But I am living proof that prayer of confession releases unexplainable, supernatural forgiveness, enough to change the course of one's life!

On that premise, I confess my sins in writing every day. I am not afraid of letting God see me as I really am because He knows the "real" me anyway. Confession or admission is agreement with God that I need help to make changes, that I know I have more work to do, and that I am sorry that I've hurt Him or anyone else.

I don't ever feel condemned during the ADMIT section of my prayer time. (If I was going to feel condemned, I would have felt that way on the first day in my relationship with God.) Somehow God allowed me to learn that to come to Him with my sins is not another blow to our relationship, but it is a part of our relationship that He desires for us to confront and deal with, *with* His help!

He knows that we are human and that we will fail or fall. We are not surprising Him with our confessions, but coming to ask for help, a way out, an escape, or an answer to our repeated shortcomings.

That is why I believe so strongly in—and am committed to—the practice of confessing my sins in writing on a daily basis. It is good for me to have accountability with God every twenty-four hours rather than

> every once in a while, or

>> when everything falls apart at once, or

>>> when things are so bad that I have no other recourse than to go to God!

What might be the results of the practice of daily admission of sin?

_____

_____

_____

_____

_____

_____

Other results might include (1) release from guilt and shame, replaced with a genuine freedom to be happy in God; (2) reexamination of our priorities and personality; (3) an inner desire to make certain changes; and (4) the qualification to be powerful and effective pray-ers (James 5:16).

If you haven't done this before or don't know where to start, I suggest being honest with God about your day (or previous day, depending on what time of day you chose to have your appointment with Him). Begin this section by reading or writing Psalm 139:23–24. Then sit quietly for a moment and see what thoughts immediately come to your mind. You might begin as if you were in a conversation with a pastor or counselor, by relating your everyday (and current day) struggles with anger, possible tempting traps, inconsistencies, lusts, or integrity issues.

I usually find myself discussing a relationship, a disagreement, or a difficulty that I am having with controlling my temper or impatience or trust. It may seem that certain confessions never change, but I consider it more like recurring weaknesses vie for a place in my life. The practice of daily confessing these sins in writing allows me to immediately see and identify any

patterns,

stubborn traits, and the

disparity between what is happening and what is my responsibility.

Have you noticed any weaknesses or specific sins that have been especially frequent or hard to overcome? List them in the space provided.

_____

_____

_____

_____

_____

_____

_____

When I have called something sin in my life rather than rationalized it as a bad habit, a mistake, or even an inherited trait, I have accepted God's—and my own—displeasure toward the offense. In admitting our shortcomings, weaknesses, and faults to God, we are agreeing with Him that we have been wrong—even sinful. By avoiding the pain and humiliation that come with the confession of sin in our lives, we are putting off the inevitable exposure of sin. I've found daily confession to be less painful, and it is a most powerful catalyst for change. To deny or avoid naming my problem as sin, I further procrastinate getting over and through the issue. Dealing with it comes when I admit my problem.

In the journal space provided, begin with Psalm 139:23–24, then sit quietly. In letter form, admit to the Lord what your struggles are today.

_____

_____

_____

_____

_____

_____

_____

_____

_____

_____

_____

_____

_____

_____

_____

_____

_____

What thoughts immediately popped into your mind of an area that you could acknowledge was less than God's best for you (for example, an argument with your child or spouse, a little white lie, withholding of forgiveness toward someone)?

_____

_____

_____

_____

_____

_____

_____

During this time in prayer, you might be moved to tears, truly ashamed of a certain situation or weakness. Crying, even sobbing, may be both healing and eventful, marking your confession as bringing you to a point of humility, regret, or remorse. But if you aren't emotionally moved, don't assume you haven't experienced the process of confession and forgiveness. Allow your written record of admission to serve as the actual moment you told God you were sorry and ready to change and you needed His help. Then watch and expectantly wait for God's help, forgiveness, and intervention to be on the way. Often the first step in making necessary changes is the admission of guilt. It seems in our helplessness, God's strength and power seem more evident and present.

Ending on a High Note

After listing any and all of the areas of my life and relationships that need to be cleansed and forgiven, I close with a paraphrase of Romans 12:1–2: "Therefore, I urge you, brothers, in view of God's mercy, to offer your bodies as living sacrifices, holy and pleasing to God—this is your spiritual act of worship. Do not conform any longer to the pattern of this world, but be transformed by the renewing of your mind. Then you will be able to test and approve what God's will is—his good, pleasing and perfect will."

After memorizing these verses, I personalized and paraphrased the words, and I pray them, "Fill me up to overflowing with an extra measure of Your Holy Spirit, O Lord! Change, renew, empower, and transform me. I am Yours. I need You. Forgive me, Lord, and make me new. Amen."

I encourage you to paraphrase these verses in your own words.

_____

_____

_____

_____

_____

_____

_____

_____

REQUESTS

One of the most exciting aspects of *My Partner Prayer Journal* is the REQUESTS section. On occasion, after giving one of my prayer workshops, I've been told that I made some Christians nervous because I got so enthusiastic when talking about the many answers to prayer. They were afraid that I was giving people false ideas about prayer. A few people even told me that I shared too many exciting answers—and not enough "no" answers—to prayer. I understood their concerns and tried to hold myself back, but part of my dilemma has been that many answers to prayer are direct results of praying *many* prayers.

Check each phrase that applies to you:

- ☐ I feel strange asking God for things that I want or desire.
- ☐ I give God all the requests that I think He puts on my heart.
- ☐ I don't ask God for anything for myself.
- ☐ I give requests to God more for myself than I do for anyone else.
- ☐ I request things of God throughout my day as they come to my mind.
- ☐ I have a prayer list where I record who and what I need to pray for.

C. S. Lewis felt that a request, by definition, is not a demand, but something that "may or may not be granted." A *request* can be defined as the act of asking for something. And the psalmist who wrote Psalm 5 prayed,

> In the morning, O LORD, you hear my voice;
>   in the morning I lay my requests before you
>   and wait in expectation (v. 3).

One of my favorite stories is of a woman in her late fifties who felt that writing down prayer requests was almost irreverent. She was concerned that a prayer list might make God out to be a Santa Claus or might become a wish list. I shared with her the benefits I had experienced with a written prayer list:

1. I didn't forget to pray for people who had asked me to pray for them.
2. I could stay focused during intercessory prayer for others instead of losing momentum by daydreaming.
3. I had written proof that—and how—God answered these prayers and couldn't chalk them up as coincidence, chance, or luck.

The woman, a godly missionary, took my challenge—perhaps initially to disprove me! One month after the workshop, she got in touch with me to say, "Of her 130 written requests, God had answered 127 of them specifically!" The excitement for both of us was not in how God had answered, but that He had answered so many of them specifically!

This illustrated that (1) *all* prayer is answered in God's way and in His timing; and (2) God answers prayer in more ways than by saying yes.

She never did tell me how God had answered those prayers, but she knew He had answered them. In E. Stanley Jones's booklet *How to Pray*, he says, "For God wants not merely to answer your prayer. He wants to make you—to make you into the kind of person through whom he can habitually answer prayer."

(In chapters 10 through 15 of this workbook, many types

of requesting prayers will be discussed at greater length. The purpose of this section is to help you develop a personal prayer list.)

As an experiment, begin a prayer request list. In *My Partner Prayer Journal* or your own journal, list all the people you love, those who need specific prayer, or any special concerns or projects. Then leave space after each person, organization, or project for additions, updates, and amplifications.

Family

_____   _____

_____   _____

_____   _____

_____   _____

_____   _____

_____   _____

Friends

_____   _____

_____   _____

_____   _____

_____   _____

_____   _____

_____   _____

Church

_____   _____

_____   _____

_____   _____

_____   _____

_____   _____

_____   _____

Pastor and Family   _____   _____

_____   _____

_____   _____

_____   _____

_____   _____

_____   _____

The President,
Congressional
Representatives,
Senators

_____   _____

_____   _____

_____   _____

_____   _____

_____   _____

_____   _____

Bosses,
Coworkers

_____   _____

_____   _____

_____   _____

_____   _____

_____   _____

_____   _____

Missionaries
(Ones You
Prayerfully and
Financially
Support)

_____   _____

_____   _____

_____   _____

_____   _____

_____   _____

Dreams or Goals   _____   _____

_____   _____

Dreams or Goals
(Cont'd)

_____   _____
_____   _____
_____   _____
_____   _____

People Who
Need Healing

_____   _____
_____   _____
_____   _____
_____   _____
_____   _____

People You Need
to Make
Amends With

_____   _____
_____   _____
_____   _____
_____   _____
_____   _____

Special Concerns

_____   _____
_____   _____
_____   _____
_____   _____

Events

_____   _____
_____   _____
_____   _____
_____   _____
_____   _____

Once you have developed a working prayer list or first draft, you can tailor the list to fit your personality and time frame. Other ideas that can be incorporated into your prayer list might include the following.

1. Create a "be" list. This is how the first page in my request list reads: Dear Lord, please cause me to be a/an

- trusting, wise woman.
- affectionate wife.
- nurturing, gentle mother.
- patient businesswoman.
- gentle, positive, fair boss.
- bold evangelist.
- concerned stranger.
- faithful friend.
- loving Christian.
- BeBe-CeCe Winans–type speaker.
- discerning leader.
- powerful mentor.
- encouraging sister and daughter.
- Spirit-led, Spirit-skilled, and Spirit-filled person.

Now develop your own "be" list, based on your relationships, responsibilities, and goals:

Dear Lord, please cause me to be a/an

_____

_____

_____

_____

_____

_____

_____

_____

_____

_____

_____

_____

_____

_____

_____.

2. Pray Scripture for yourself or others. You might choose to pray for yourself,

Lord, I humble myself before You (1 Peter 5:6).

I commit my every way to You, Lord . . .
    my appetites,
    my attitudes,
    my anxieties,
    my actions,
    my aspirations,
    my anticipations, even
    my anger,
that You, O Lord, might make my life shine like the dawn, the justice of Your cause like the noonday sun (Ps. 37:5–6).

Lord, please give me Spirit-filled confidence as a Christian woman in the nineties. Give me Your Spirit, who exudes power, love, and self-control (2 Tim. 1:7).

In praying for others, you might choose a passage such as Colossians 1:9–11:

For this reason we also, since the day we heard it, do not cease to pray for you, and to ask that you may be filled with the knowledge of His will in all wisdom and spiritual understanding; that you may walk worthy of the Lord, fully pleasing Hirn, being fruitful in every good work and increasing in the knowledge of God; strengthened with all might, according to His glorious power, for all patience and longsuffering with joy (NKJV).

3. Add photographs or maps to your prayer list. You can paste photos or maps on the page where you list your kids and spouse, in-laws, missionaries, or even unsaved relatives. To see their faces and identify where they are in ministry might increase your ability to focus during your requesting prayers.

4. Divide the list into categories and pray for certain categories on specific days if time is a factor and your request list is long, but important. Every day pray for family members, yourself, and any urgent request or daily concerns. On Monday—missionaries; Tuesday—pastor and family, the church; Wednesday—friends and extended family members; Thursday—people who need healing and recovery; Friday—coworkers; and Saturday and Sunday—new acquaintances and requests.

Many attributes will naturally develop in your life because of the REQUESTS section of *My Partner Prayer Journal.* The first will be *patience.* Though I have not come right out and asked God to develop this in me, it is one of the virtues that does blossom (or is squeezed out of you) as a result of having a prayer list. Though some prayers are an swered in one day or even in an hour, many will take months or even years to come to pass. As you learn to persevere in prayer, the maturing quality of patience will become your constant companion (or thorn!).

On a scale of 1 to 10, rate yourself on how patient you think you are (1 being never patient, 10 being always patient).

1   2   3   4   5   6   7   8   9   10

Would you like to be more patient?

☐ Yes   ☐ No   ☐ Not right now

A second significant result of requesting prayer is your experience of God's *rescue*. If you have experienced God's dramatic intervention in your life, you will find yourself much more fervent, diligent, and passionate to intercede in prayer for the rescue of another. Sometimes you might not even know a person you are asked to pray for, but because you believe God does rescue, you are compelled to pray. Psalm 34 encourages us to pray, "I sought the LORD, and he answered me; / he delivered me from all my fears" (v. 4).

In the space provided, describe a time when (1) you felt rescued by a prayer, or (2) your prayers helped someone else.

_____

_____

_____

_____

_____

_____

_____

_____

_____

_____

Answers are absolute results of prayer. Now, how God answers might be different from what you anticipated, but while waiting for God to answer, have a Psalm 5:3 attitude:

> In the morning, O LORD, you hear my voice;
>   in the morning I lay my requests before you
>   and wait in expectation.

Expecting God to answer a prayer is not being
    anxious,
        distrustful, or
            doubtful.
It is a confident trust. It is waiting with the attitude found in Revelation 3:7: "There is no door that can be shut that God wants open and no door that can be opened that God wants shut."

Do you have trouble waiting for God to answer you? If you do, explain why.

_____

_____

_____

_____

_____

_____

Do you think that God answers *all* prayer?

_____

_____

_____

_____

_____

Are you waiting for an answer even now? Describe the situation.

_____

_____

_____

_____

_____

I regularly discuss the *yearnings* or desires of my heart on my prayer list. I use this section of my notebook to pray specifically about my dreams and goals. Psalm 37:4 reminds me to "delight yourself also in the LORD, / and He shall give you the desires of your heart" (NKJV).

What does Psalm 37:4 mean to you?

_____

_____

_____

_____

_____

When I am talking to God about the desires of my heart, I am not trying to make Him give me what I want; I am asking Him to confirm and bring about the dreams I believe He has put in my heart from before all time. Though those dreams have stretched out over years before coming to pass, many have been fulfilled.

Another attribute that has grown stronger and remains a high priority in my life is my *enthusiasm for evangelism*. Because my love for the Lord is strong, when I place on my prayer list the names of new acquaintances, unsaved family members, coworkers, or neighbors, I am motivated to pray that they will come to know God's love. Even ideas on what to share, how to share, and where to invite those with whom I'm witnessing will come to mind during my time in prayer for them.

List the names of some unsaved family members, friends, and acquaintances you would like to see come to know Christ and His love.

_____

_____

_____

_____

_____

_____

_____

In addition, place these people on your prayer list, and ask God to show you if there is anything He would have you do or say to them that might draw them closer to Him.

Taking *responsibility* and initiative has also been a direct result of my prayer list. I heard Charles Stanley say, "Don't pray about anything you wouldn't want God to do through you!" I've taken that to heart when I put people, projects, and needs (mine or others') on my request list. During prayer I am prompted to ask myself, Can I be the one to send the extra money that they need? Should I invite them to church? How can I help my son to read the Bible rather than just pray that he reads his Bible?

How do you feel about taking responsibility for your prayers?

_____

_____

_____

_____

_____

_____

Does any situation come to mind, even now, in which you could take some new responsibility?

_____

_____

_____

_____

All those wonderful attributes—and more—develop as you regularly pray from a prayer list.

If you have further questions about prayer, look up the following verses to help you answer these questions:

Can you ask too much or too often? (See Phil. 4:6.)

_____

_____

_____

_____

Does God get mad when we ask? (See James 1:5; 4:2.)

_____

_____

_____

_____

Can you pray too long for something? (See Luke 18:1–8.)

_____

_____

_____

_____

Are there prerequisites to having prayer answered? (See Pss. 37:4; 66:18; 84:11; James 4:3.)

_____

_____

_____

_____

Can/will my prayers make a difference? (See Pss. 15; 24; James 5:16.)

_____

_____

_____

_____

Though much about prayer remains a mystery, I personally am helped by C. S. Lewis's remarks, "When we are praying, the thought will often cross our minds that (if only we knew it) the event is already decided one way or the other. I believe this to be no good reason for ceasing our prayers. The event certainly has been decided—in a sense it was decided 'before all worlds.' But one of the things that really cause it to happen may be this very prayer that we are now offering."

In the space provided, record your reaction to Lewis's quote.

_____

_____

_____

_____

_____

_____

_____

_____

THANKS

Be joyful always; pray continually; give thanks in all circumstances, for this is God's will for you in Christ Jesus (1 Thess. 5:16–18).

When was the last time you thanked the Lord for a specific answer to prayer, recognizing His intervention or giving Him credit for something wonderful that occurred rather than crediting that "something" to luck, chance, or coincidence?

This THANKS section at the end of My P.A.R.T. in prayer is meant to be easy and relational. It can be as comfortable as sending a note to someone you really appreciate, acknowledging kindness, rescue, thoughtfulness, or financial aid—and as short as a one-line thank-you note.

When we begin to look at life through the scope of prayers that are lifted up *to* God and then answered *by* God, we no longer have to use the words *luck, chance,* and *coincidence!*

List three occurrences in the past few weeks that you feel were orchestrated by God.

_____

_____

_____

_____

_____

_____

_____

_____

_____

Have you thanked God for them yet? If not, take time now to do that.

_____

_____

_____

_____

_____

_____

_____

_____

_____

A thank-You note to God is a purposeful acknowledgment to Him that you noticed His hand in your life. When you articulate in writing on a daily basis what you believe He has done for you, you have eye-opening, black-and-white proof that God is—and wants to be—intimately involved in your life. The THANKS section is a perfect place to *thank God specifically for answers to prayer* on a daily basis. To look back at it at the end of every month or year is a great refresher course on how much God loves you.

Up until now, what priority has thanking God had in your prayer life? (Check one.)

☐ A very big part—I thank Him constantly.

☐ A somewhat significant part—I thank Him occasionally.

☐ Rather small—I thank Him for only a few things when I pray.

☐ Not much—I rarely thank Him specifically for anything.

Rather than check off answers to prayer on your requests list, take the time and make the effort to daily examine the blessings in your life. Ask yourself, How did God work in my life today? What is an answer to prayer that I have waited for that God answered today and in what way? In what small way did I sense God's love, touch, favor, or comfort today?

Make a habit of ending your P.A.R.T. in prayer with an affirmation of your love for God. Use the words, "I love You, Lord."

In the space provided, describe a way that He came into your life, intervened on your behalf, or helped you out *in the last year*.

_____

_____

_____

_____

_____

_____

_____

_____

_____

Can you remember a time *in the last month* that you asked God for something for yourself or for another and He responded? Explain that answer to prayer.

_____

_____

_____

_____

_____

_____

_____

_____

_____

How *in this past week* have you sensed God's presence, direction, help, nudge, or answer to prayer?

_____

_____

_____

_____

_____

_____

Try to thank Him for more than material blessings.
Thank You, Lord, for . . .

Emotional (for example, my husband's love for me, his concern for my hurt feelings, etc.)

_____

_____

_____

_____

Physical (for example, that my son, Jake, passed his driver's test)

_____

_____

_____

_____

_____

Spiritual (for example, that I'm growing more quick to forgive)

_____

_____

_____

_____

_____

Mental (for example, that the writing of this book is not as
difficult as that of the last one)

_____

_____

_____

_____

_____

Now, take those four P.A.R.T.s in prayer, and build a letter
of PRAISE, ADMIT, REQUESTS, and THANKS to God. In
this letter, you might tell Him how much you appreciated
His hand on your life or how safe it made you feel when He
took care of a situation for you. Be honest with your feelings
and thoughts, and be sure to include your confession and
requests! Most important, see this letter as an acknowledgment to God (and perhaps to yourself) that He is the One who

is in control of your life, opens the doors, and deserves glory and credit for the answers!

CHAPTER 8

MY PARTNER PRAYER JOURNAL: GOD'S PART

LISTENING

God's PART to me in *My Partner Prayer Journal* begins with the section called LISTENING. Perhaps the most awkward and least natural area in prayer for me has been the LISTENING section. Admittedly, this area of prayer has not come as easily as the REQUESTS or THANKS sections of my journal.

To discern the sound of God's voice, to read His Word and believe that He is speaking to us, develops over time.

How confident are you that a person is able to hear God's voice?

☐ Extremely   ☐ Very   ☐ Somewhat

☐ Not very   ☐ Not at all

I have never believed that any part of a Christian's walk is meant to be so spiritual that it is impossible to grasp. But some areas will be more difficult to master; they will take more practice, study, and research to understand them fully.

Have you ever felt as if you were hearing God's voice? In the space provided, describe what it sounded like to you.

_____

_____

_____

_____

_____

_____

_____

After regular attempts of listening to God, I became convinced that God did want to speak to me through His Word, Holy Spirit, and other messengers. Soon I noticed a certain thread during my listening time.

God's voice sounded like Scripture! Usually, a verse I had recently heard or previously memorized would pop into my head to nudge me (1) away from doing something wrong, or (2) toward a great idea on how to accomplish or create something new or special.

In Jerry Bridges's book, *Pursuit of Holiness*, he detailed these ways that a believer can best hear God's voice:

- Hearing Scripture used in sermons
- Reading the Bible regularly for knowing God's viewpoint on all aspects of life
- Studying the Scriptures intently for special counsel
- Memorizing key passages for immediate recall

I have regularly used these guidelines to help me discern if I have heard God's counsel in a matter.

If you are a beginning listener, I suggest that you set aside specific times to listen to God—and not talk. Even older or seasoned listeners make that a habit. As you become more familiar with God's voice during planned listening times, you will eventually be able to discern God's voice throughout your whole day—whether you are praying, driving your car, sitting in church, or walking your dog.

I have read a number of books on this subject because it is an area where I know that I can improve and increase my knowledge. Books by Andrew Murray, such as *The Prayer Life, Inner Life, Confession, Forgiveness,* and *Christ in the School of Prayer,* were definitely great teachers to me, opening my eyes to the inner life and spiritual disciplines of listening and meditating. A. W. Tozer took the invisible concept of listening to God and made it more tangible:

> I think the average person's progression will be something like this . . . First, a sound as a presence walking in the garden. Then a voice, more intelligible, but still far from clear. Then

the happy moment when the Spirit begins to illuminate the Scriptures and that which had only been a sound or at best a voice now becomes an intelligible word, warm and intimate and as clear as the word of a dear friend.

How does the concept of listening to God presented in this quote by A. W. Tozer make you feel about the possibility of hearing God's voice? Explain your feelings.

_____

_____

_____

_____

_____

_____

_____

Is this type of two-way conversation with God a desire of yours?

☐ Yes   ☐ Somewhat   ☐ Not sure   ☐ No

Upon listening to God, we have the equally interesting opportunity to obey Him. I recently spoke with a woman who was struggling with immorality in her life, and she said that she suffered from a great deal of confusion and depression. After I inquired if she had been talking to the Lord, she confessed that she could not "get herself" to pray anymore. Though it was hard, I had to ask her, "Could it be that you are afraid to hear what God might ask you to do?" Through her tears came the answer: "Yes."

List some of the reasons you might not want to listen to God's voice.

_____

_____

_____

_____

_____

_____

_____

Begin the LISTENING section with a silent or written prayer, asking God to speak to you through His Holy Spirit. Because you have previously spoken to God in the PRAISE, ADMIT, REQUESTS, and THANKS sections of *My Partner Prayer Journal* or your journal concerning your needs, specific decisions you have to make, or a problem that is bothering you, ask Him if He has any direction, counsel, or advise for you. Then listen. Be silent and attentive to the next thoughts or Scripture verses that come into your mind.

As they are coming *or* after you have listened, write down those thoughts and verses.

_____

_____

_____

_____

_____

_____

If a verse comes to mind, but you are not certain where it is found in the Bible, look in a concordance to find the exact reference. Often I will read the entire chapter where the verse that came to mind is located. If those verses have direct application to the prayers I have previously prayed in my journal, I even underline, date, and highlight them in my Bible.

Very often I am encouraged, comforted, corrected, or directed by the thoughts or Scriptures that come to mind. E. Stanley Jones concluded, "The impulses that come out of the prayer hour are usually true impulses of the Spirit. Some would say these impulses are of the spirit, but those of us who try this two-way living know that you cannot tell where your spirit ends and His Spirit begins. They are now flowing back and forth into each other. The Spirit stimulates our spirit into Spirit-led activities."

Open your Bible to the proverb that is today's date. Jot down any Scripture verses that you feel might be speaking to you today.

_____

_____

_____

_____

_____

_____

_____

_____

_____

_____

Almost daily, this LISTENING section has been one of the ways God has *confirmed* or *affirmed* a decision that I was making or a direction that I was taking. But I have been careful never to use the LISTENING section as a "stand alone." I believe that God will speak to me through His Word, His Spirit, *and* people in authority over me (for example, pastor, Bible study teacher, husband, etc.). As I lay my requests before Him and wait for His response, I find that God will use this section, in addition to other ways, to guide me. If just one area strongly directs me, I will wait until the other areas line up in agreement. If all areas except one give me a "green light," I will often ask God to give me confirmation by putting that last piece in place.

My husband always tells me, "Becky, don't tell people that *God* told you to do this. Tell them that you *think, believe,* or *sense* that God is directing you in this or that way, sharing with them the verses and other confirmations that cause you to believe that." The wisdom behind this counsel is (1) to protect me from impulsively making a decision based only on one incident, verse, or listening time, and (2) to responsibly model *how* to listen to God.

Because the listening area of our prayer time is possibly the one area that people understand the least and misinterpret the most, confidence in listening to God's voice will come only as we practice, study, and spend time listening to Him. Watching how a situation unfolds will be our best teacher in how well we heard God's voice.

Almost every day, you should be able to hear God speak to you through His Word and His Spirit. His Word and voice are not spoken or whispered to you to give you only *big* answers. You might hear daily whispers such as, "I love you," or "I understand," for a period of time. When you are listening, God might give you an idea to do something for someone else or suggest that you call someone who needs encouragement. In the listening time, you might be encouraged to send a note to someone, forgiving him or thanking her. Remember, your best guideline in discerning if you have heard God is that what you heard should always agree or line up with His Word.

John 10:3, 5 says, "He calls his own sheep by name and leads them out. . . . They will never follow a stranger; in fact, they will run away from him because they do not recognize a stranger's voice." The more time you spend listening to God, the easier it will be to hear and recognize His voice. John 10 says the sheep follow the Shepherd because they *know* His voice. If you are having trouble not only listening to God but also following God, then perhaps this is the section you should heartily dig into, learn about, develop, and practice.

Sit quietly for two to three minutes. Focus on the King, and jot down any impressions, thoughts, or verses that come to mind.

_____

_____

_____

_____

_____

_____

_____

_____

MESSAGES

In this section of *My Partner Prayer Journal* or your journal, record the verses, illustrations, and points of

sermons,

Bible studies,

small group meetings,

Christian radio messages, and

discipleship training classes

that encourage, correct, and motivate you.

In the space provided, write down the most memorable lesson you have ever learned from a pastor, a Bible study, or a similar source.

_____

_____

_____

_____

_____

_____

_____

_____

_____

One of the exciting, but mysterious aspects of the MESSAGE section is to believe that the words, stories, and Scriptures, given by these teachers, are from God to you. In making and taking these notes, you allow God to confirm an idea that you had, to correct a wrongful thought you might have been dwelling on, or to direct, convict, or possibly warn you.

So often we'll forget an important Scripture ten minutes after a sermon, limiting its ability to challenge us throughout the rest of the day or week. But if we have written it down in the MESSAGE section, we can go back and refer to it. If you've really been encouraged by a message, writing down what you heard will enable you to share what you've learned with family and friends.

When you take your journal with you to teaching times, you are going with an attitude of expectancy, anticipating that God will speak to you. And if your attitude is one of anticipation of God's words, you can also expect to be challenged to leave a different person from what you were when you entered. If you come prepared to hear a message to invite God's Holy Spirit to bring change and hope into your life, you will never be disappointed!

Have you ever felt like the speaker's works were especially for you? Describe what happened.

_____

_____

_____

_____

_____

_____

_____

To keep accurate accounts of what I've heard, who was speaking, and where I was when I heard it, I date each page and put the title of the message and the speaker's name at the top of each page. Then I write down key verses, the outline, and points the speaker makes.

Next, I say to myself, Knowing what I've been struggling with, what I'm afraid of, what I've been praying about, or what relationship I'm concerned about, I feel God used this message to _____

_____

_____

(Fill in the blank with your impressions.)

This section has

- increased my knowledge of God.
- challenged me to change an area of my life.
- made me more willing to give.
- given me a few good ideas for my own talks by building on what I've heard others say.

Keep extra paper or journals on hand because this section will fill up quickly. You might even encourage your pastor (as mine does) to put an outline of the sermon in the Sunday bulletin. This not only helps you to follow along, but it also helps you stay focused on the sermon.

NEW TESTAMENT

The whole Bible was given to us by inspiration from God and is useful to teach us what is true and to make us realize what is wrong in our lives; it straightens us out and helps us do what is right (2 Tim. 3:16 TLB).

I made a commitment to read the Bible on a daily basis during my first year as a Christian. Someone got me on a bus to hear a speaker at a convention center who asked attendees, after many convincing hours of teaching, if they would like to make a decision to read their Bibles for at least five minutes a day. Along with everyone else, I stood up. (And our church was wise enough to follow us up!)

Over and over, week after week, our pastor reminded us of our five-minutes-a-day decision until daily Bible reading was a habit, not just a good intention. Fortunately, because all of my Christian friends were attempting to acquire the same discipline, we struggled together, and most of us from that church and "era" have eighteen years of five-minutes-(or more)-a-day Bible reading under our belts (and in our hearts and minds)!

Choose the statement that best describes you:
- ☐ I read the Bible daily without fail.
- ☐ I read the Bible three or four times a week.
- ☐ I read the Bible only when I have time or feel a pressing need.
- ☐ I read the Bible rarely, if ever.
- ☐ I used to read the Bible often, but I haven't picked it up lately.
- ☐ I have never made a decision to read the Bible daily.

If you have not previously read through the New Testament—chapter by chapter—I suggest that you start here and now. Begin in Matthew, a chapter a day, until you get to the end of Revelation. And if you forget to read one day (or even a week), don't try to catch up—just pick up where you left off.

One absolutely foolproof method of getting through the Bible in a year is to use the *Change Your Life Daily*™ Bible, which is offered in many favorite translations. The *Change Your Life Daily*™ Bible, is divided into 365 days, dated so that you don't forget where you left off, and comes packaged with either the New and Old Testaments together or just the New Testament. And the *Change Your Life Daily*™ Bible, is a perfect fit with the last part of *My Partner Prayer Journal*, L.M.N.O.P.

While reading in the New Testament, I write out verses that are particularly comforting or encouraging to me during my prayer time. I make notes on how those verses related to me on that day, and I often underline, date, and highlight them in my Bible.

Look up the following verses, and note how important and influential the Word of God is meant to be in our lives if we would just allow it!

Psalm 119:9

_____

_____

_____

_____

_____

_____

Hebrews 4:12

_____
_____
_____
_____
_____
_____

2 Timothy 3:16

_____
_____
_____
_____
_____

Jerry Bridges said, "Like a good coach, the Word of God is our trainer and teacher." Have you been getting a good workout lately? Explain.

_____
_____
_____
_____
_____
_____
_____
_____
_____
_____

Have a plan when you read the Bible. There are many Bible studies, study guides, workbooks, guidelines, and monthly magazines available for you to follow—or check with your local Christian bookstore, youth pastor, parent, or small group leader to give you great ideas on what would be a good fit for you.

Have a Bible that you can underline, highlight, and write in. Take it with you whenever you attend a meeting, retreat, or service. Mark dates, places, and circumstances next to a verse that is meaningful to you. Later, as you reread that passage, it will remind you of how God provided for you at a difficult or exciting time in your life. Remember, verses that stand out may be either comforting or uncomfortable.

Have—or borrow—a dictionary, a Bible dictionary, a concordance, and a commentary for the times you run into passages that you don't understand. When you come across a verse you want to remember, list it in the back of your Bible, making a personal commentary of favorite verses.

I would like to set a goal here and now:
- ☐ Read the Bible every day for the rest of my life.
- ☐ Buy a devotional, Bible commentary or dictionary, or anything else that might enhance my prayer time.
- ☐ Begin to mark dates and events in my Bible.
- ☐ Start recording verses each day that I feel are speaking to me.
- ☐ Begin to memorize Scripture as part of my daily devotions.

If you made a goal (or goals), write the date: _____.

OLD TESTAMENT

Your word I have hidden in my heart,
That I might not sin against You (Ps. 119:11 NKJV).

I rejoice in following your statutes
  as one rejoices in great riches.
I meditate on your precepts
  and consider your ways.
I delight in your decrees;
  I will not neglect your word (Ps. 119:14–16).

Don't be fooled by the word *old*. The Lord's mercies are new every morning, and so is the freshness of His Word.

In the past, I have thought of the Old Testament in this way (or ways):
  ☐ Fascinating and relevant to my life today
  ☐ An important part in the understanding of Christianity
  ☐ A mystery I have never checked into
  ☐ Totally irrelevant to today's world
  ☐ Just a bunch of stories I don't understand

The Old Testament is the Word of God written prior to the coming of Jesus Christ, the promised Messiah. It is broken down into books of History, Law, Poetry, and Prophets. These books tell many stories of God's love, forgiveness, direction, and provision for His people, Israel. You can relate to the teachings and principles through analogies and parables.

The Old Testament overflows with messages and meaning for Christians today and grounds our faith in facts of history. In addition to affirming our faith, Psalm 119:165 declares, "Great peace have those who love Your law, / And nothing causes them to stumble" (NKJV). The promises of the Old Testament reach deep into our hearts, filling us with the hope of God. Again and again I experience increased faith and hope as I read in the Old Testament. Contrary to what some people think, the Old Testament is not outdated or irrelevant for today's Christian.

Seek guidance on where you should read in the Old Testament if you are hesitant. Many daily guides, commentaries, devotionals, topical systems, and study guides are available to help you. Again, an excellent tool is *The One Year Bible*, which makes it easy to read through the entire Bible in a year. Each day's reading includes passages from the Old Testament and New Testament, a psalm, and a few verses from Proverbs.

Read a chapter a day from the Bible or a few verses at a time—whatever you think you can keep up with. Stay at it. If you've stopped reading, pick your Bible up today and start reading. If you've completely lost interest in the method you are currently using, then change gears. At all costs, stay in the Word of God—it is God's voice to you!

Read the following Scriptures, and record any impression you have about the need for God's Word in your daily life.

Psalm 119

_____

_____

_____

_____

_____

_____

Joshua 1:8

_____

_____

_____

_____

_____

Psalm 119:2

_____

_____

_____

_____

_____

Psalm 19:11

_____

_____

_____

_____

_____

Again, both Old and New Testaments are meant for every Christian—young or old—to read. Be diligent to search for, acquire, and pursue a regular, daily Bible reading plan. It is an absolute part of your two-way conversation with God.

PROVERBS

The book of Proverbs is for all

*P*eople; advising us how to make
*R*ight choices and providing us the
*O*pportunity to grow, with pertinent
*V*erses for
*E*very day.
*R*ead through all thirty-one chapters each month. Your
    hunger for the
*B*ible will grow, and God's
*S*pirit will teach you wisdom and godliness.

Proverbs is a very practical book of the Bible for believers today! It has instruction and warning about sex, marriage, hard and lazy workers, adultery, gossip, speaking the truth, befriending the wrong people, being wise or being a fool, getting drunk, and making money. (Who hasn't faced one of these issues in the past year?)

Proverbs 1:4 states that the proverbs are "to give prudence to the simple, / to the young man knowledge and discretion" (NKJV). Most of us would admit to struggling with temptations that are flirting with us everywhere we turn—in the office, at school, at home, on television, at the movies, or on the radio. Perhaps a proverb-a-day can be protection from the world, which may be attacking you from every angle. The Proverbs are meant to bring God's viewpoint and His wisdom into your daily life.

Do you feel that you could use prudence, knowledge, and discretion in your life?

☐ Yes, definitely!　　☐ Sure, I think so!
☐ No, I don't think so!

The following ideas are options to bring the book of Proverbs into your prayer life.

Option 1: For the most studious, read a chapter of Proverbs each day. There are thirty-one chapters, so you can repeat the whole book on a monthly basis. Take notes or just pick one verse each day and jot it down in the PROVERBS section of *My Partner Prayer Journal* or your journal.

Option 2: For the rest of us, read a few verses every day, making your way through the entire book of Proverbs at your own pace. To make it effective, jot down at least one verse each day that applies to your life. In addition, ask God to give you wisdom and strength in the areas you might be relating to or struggling with at this time.

Option 3: Memorize a proverb that seems particularly pertinent to you. Write out the verse in this section of your journal, and review it daily. It might also help to write the verse on an index card and carry it with you, so you can recite it several times during the day.

If you would like to, set a goal (by writing it out on page 130) to practice one or more of these options daily.

_____

_____

_____

_____

_____

_____

_____

_____

_____

_____

_____

_____

TO DO

Have you ever been distracted and interrupted while praying by remembering something you needed to do?

☐ Always ☐ Often ☐ Rarely ☐ Never

The TO DO section, as a part of *My Partner Prayer Journal,* is more a necessity than it might appear. So often during time with God, I am reminded through a verse or admit prayer to call someone, send a note, pay a debt, or buy a gift. At other times while praying, I might receive a great, innovative idea. What I've learned is not to get up at that moment and begin to do it because that will stop my prayer time. Instead, I jot down the note in a dated, organized place (the TO DO section of *My Partner Prayer Journal*—see example on following pages) so that I can look at, think about, and do it later.

I frequently scribble four to six notes during my prayer hour. Two or three of the to do's are for today. I do two more later that week. And one or two of the ideas I put on a long-term list of good ideas for when the right time arises.

Is there anything that never seems to go on your "to do" list but often comes to mind during prayer (for example, send flowers to _____ , send a check to _____ , don't forget to return _____ , etc.)? List any TO DO'S that God might be nudging you about even now.

_____

_____

_____

_____

_____

_____

_____

_____

_____

_____

_____

_____

_____

_____

_____

_____

THE DESIGN FOR PRAYER

DATE:

MONTH   DAY   YEAR

5:00 AM	
:30	
6:00	
:30	
7:00	
:30	
8:00	
:30	
9:00	
:30	
10:00	
:30	
11:00	
:30	
12:00 PM	
:30	
1:00	
:30	
2:00	
:30	
3:00	
:30	
4:00	
:30	
5:00	
:30	
6:00	
:30	
7:00	
:30	
8:00	
:30	
9:00	
:30	
10:00	
:30	
11:00	
:30	

CALL:

TELEPHONE NUMBER

☐
☐
☐
☐
☐
☐
☐

LETTERS TO WRITE:

☐
☐
☐
☐
☐

OCCASION
CARDS TO SEND:

DATE

☐
☐
☐

EXPENSES
TO RECORD:

AMOUNT

MILEAGE:

FROM   TO   TOTAL

_____ =_____

_____ =_____

DROP OFF:

- ☐ _____
- ☐ _____
- ☐ _____

PICK UP:

- ☐ _____
- ☐ _____
- ☐ _____

RETURN:

- ☐ _____
- ☐ _____
- ☐ _____

PLAN FOR:

- ☐ _____
- ☐ _____
- ☐ _____
- ☐ _____

PRAY FOR:

- ☐ _____
- ☐ _____
- ☐ _____
- ☐ _____

"TO DO"

- ☐ _____
- ☐ _____
- ☐ _____
- ☐ _____
- ☐ _____
- ☐ _____
- ☐ _____
- ☐ _____
- ☐ _____
- ☐ _____

MEMORY VERSE: _____

_____

_____

_____

PART FOUR

DELIGHTS, DESIRES, DREAMS

CHAPTER 9

POWERFUL PRAYER PRINCIPLES

Sherwood Eddy said, "You can only prove the reality of prayer by praying!" And I agree! I can tell you of many answers to prayer that might inspire you to pray, but you will be more desirous and fervent to pray when you have seen God work in your life as a result of your own prayers.

Early in the first year of my hourly appointments with God, it was obvious that a supernatural power was being released when I prayed. This increased my faith and kept me accountable and motivated to meeting with God. As I would face a new day, I was just as sure that I would face a new adventure. Prayer was the time and place where my dreams and ideas turned into more—they became written conversations with the King about my whole life.

On any given day, an answer to prayer would come in the

form of an idea, phone call, or letter, changing my course or direction. I have to admit that sometimes I would pray out of curiosity, wondering what might happen next, how God would answer my request, or what unexpected response might come.

Does what I've described in the above paragraph sound different from your personal experience with prayer? Identify the ways it has been different or similar or how you hope your prayers might become.

_____

_____

_____

_____

_____

_____

_____

_____

_____

_____

Because I was experiencing so many answers to prayer, I decided to take the next discovery step in prayer and research the patterns, principles, and paths in prayer.

First, I took the concordance of my Bible and looked up every verse that had the word *ask, believe,* or *pray* in it. (Of course, that was before concordances were on computer programs, which would have saved me a lot of time!) Upon looking up and writing out these verses, I was amazed, but mostly motivated by their directives. Jesus spoke many of the verses. The verses repeatedly indicated that God encouraged us to ask Him in prayer and to believe Him for the answers to our prayers.

After compiling this list, I was even more convinced to pray. In fact, I thought that I'd be absolutely negligent if I didn't pray.

Within months after I made the decision to pray for an hour a day, my insecurities and misconceptions about prayer seemed to be quickly fading away. To my surprise, I was developing a list of every reason under the sun for which to pray!

To get you started, look up the following verses.

Matthew 6:33

_____

_____

_____

_____

Matthew 7:7–8

_____

_____

_____

_____

Philippians 4:6

_____

_____

_____

_____

Matthew 21:22

_____

_____

_____

_____

My discovery reminded me of an archaeological find where what was once hidden had been uncovered to reveal a power source. Prayer is an inestimable resource for the believer to access, use, have, and draw from at any time.

At first, I was skeptical of the "too good to be true" sound of each verse, but I began to categorize, test, assess, and try out each verse, not only for its validity, but also for its application within my life. I could not stop myself from reminiscing about the daring faith I possessed during my early Christian days. Those were the days when I prayed about everything and believed that God wanted to do "immeasurably more than all [I could] ask or imagine" (Eph. 3:20).

Complete the following: My opinion about prayer is
☐ growing more hopeful.
☐ not changing at all.
☐ still not totally formed.

In addition, I was compelled to read more about the lives and experiences of other prayer discoverers, such as George Mueller, Leonard Ravenhill, and Wesley Duewel. I read _more_ of Andrew Murray's classics on prayer than I had previously devoured. (Again, I must bring one fact to light: If you knew me well, you would be certain that I would not voluntarily search out books by very old or very dead people on a subject that held potentially boring content.) It seemed inconceivable to me that I would be experiencing similar finds as the theologians and desert fathers of the past, yet my "ooohs" and "aaahhs" and "oh, yeses" came from relating to every word I was reading. Again, I found the adventure in prayer to be more life-changing than any single experience in my Christian life, except for my conversion.

To make sense of my findings—and explain them in contemporary words—I decided to organize, categorize, and name each principle and pattern that I was discovering about prayer. I initially developed a list of principles that I called my six powerful prayer principles. I narrowed down the verses into six categories by observing how Jesus prayed, how the Old and New Testament heroes talked to God, and how prayer was practiced throughout the Psalms. The following six patterns in prayer became the biblical principles that undergirded my prayer life:

1. Receiving (or asking) prayer
2. Revealing prayer
3. Believing prayer
4. Interceding prayer
5. Agreeing prayer
6. Persevering prayer

Let's explore these principles and patterns together.

CHAPTER 10

RECEIVING PRAYER

You want something but don't get it. You kill and covet, but you cannot have what you want. You quarrel and fight. You do not have, because you do not ask God. When you ask, you do not receive, because you ask with wrong motives, that you may spend what you get on your pleasures.—James 4:2–3

Be anxious for nothing, but in everything by prayer and supplication, with thanksgiving, let your requests be made known to God.—Philippians 4:6 NKJV

Shortly after discovering prayer as my daily opportunity for connecting with God, I began to read afresh the Scriptures *about* prayer. I was absolutely struck with the reality that if I took these verses at face value, I could be living a much more adventurous Christian life.

After reading and meditating on the verses at the beginning of this chapter, I quickly gained a new freedom in asking of God, giving up my previous misconceptions that I might be bothering Him or that receiving or asking prayer was selfish. Instead, I began to believe that Jesus was inviting me to ask of Him, as He spoke in Matthew 7:7–8: "Ask and it will be given to you; seek and you will find; knock and the door will be opened to you. For everyone who asks receives; he who seeks finds; and to him who knocks, the door will be opened."

I gained a fresh perspective on prayer from reading and rereading the whole list of New Testament and Old Testament verses that I had collected. They gave me the courage and encouragement to ask in prayer, but they also gave me practical guidelines. I was very comfortable asking God in prayer, but I was also reminded that before I asked, I should check or consider my motives.

Many people are afraid to ask God for a request, fearing that they might bother, offend, or overstep a boundary with Him. From the moment I began to freely ask God in prayer, the results have been exciting! The answers have been so exciting, I sometimes want to classify them as miracles.

In receiving or asking prayer, we often have the opportunity to ask God for what might seem impossible. When we believe that God will intervene and answer impossible prayers, we have the faith to pray. Asking is not putting God on the line to perform. It is not *telling* Him to do a miracle; it is *asking* Him to intervene, then watching to see what He chooses to do.

Perhaps that is why many believers don't ask of God. Perhaps they do not believe that God can, will, or wants to do a miracle (intervene in a situation, open a door, heal an illness) on their behalf.

Have you considered these questions?
- Do I believe in miracles?
- What do I consider a miracle?
- Is a miracle something that appears to be impossible, yet unexplainably becomes possible?

_____

_____

_____

_____

_____

_____

_____

In the "Mounds of Miracles" chapter in *Let Prayer Change Your Life,* I shared the following story of how our Ohio house sold in one day:

The sheer thrill of moving from the midwestern cloudy days, flat terrain, and cold, cold winters to the year-round sunny, warm days of southern California seemed too good to be true! But when reality struck, six weeks was an unbelievably short period of time to sell the house and cars, tie up loose ends, and get in as much time with family and friends as possible— not to mention taking forty-eight high schoolers on a "Florida Breakaway" in the midst of it all.

Perhaps all those reasons prodded me to ask the Lord for something special. It took us two of the six available weeks just to get our house marketable—painting and even putting up new drapes—so when it came to actually listing and selling our home, acquiring a Realtor *seemed* out of the question, unless someone was to stay behind or leave an outsider with the burden of selling an empty house and taking care of all the many details of a house sale. So I simply asked, "Lord, would You sell our house in a day?"

I had been reading in Isaiah during the months prior to the big turn of events in our lives, and the chapters were full of promises and prompting to dream and soar and "not be afraid." They were words to put hope in while still waiting for God's plan to unfold.

Chapters 40—60 of Isaiah were marked and dated constantly with comments relating to evangelism, discipleship, and being a messenger of the gospel. As hope gained a foothold that it was indeed God's will for us to move to California, I felt it was not wrong to at least *ask* for His supernatural intervention.

On a Tuesday, I called the newspaper to put in an ad for a "House for Sale," with all the details. The telephone solicitor asked if we'd be having an open house—a one-day showing. I said, "No." She continued to push me, oddly, until I had narrowed it down to that coming Sunday for 1:00 to 5:00 P.M.— the "norm" she suggested for an open house.

Then I began to ask my friends to pray, "Would you pray with me and ask God to sell my house in a day?" Some jumped on the bandwagon with great anticipation, and others chided me by saying, "Well, you know, Becky, God doesn't always do things like that a second time."

Five years earlier, we had outgrown our little home after the birth of our son. With the same inkling that God was prompting, I felt we should put our first little house up for sale on the Fourth of July (not a real hot day for house sales) with a specific, nonnegotiable selling price and without the assistance of a Realtor. I believed God wanted our house up for sale that day! When I suggested we do that, my husband thought I was being a bit impulsive, but with his permission, that morning I hammered a big FOR SALE sign into our front lawn. Unbelievably we had a buyer for our full asking price that afternoon. Therefore, when a few of my friends didn't seem to believe God would answer that prayer . . . I asked them not to pray at all, because I believed God had been giving me Scriptures and an inner confidence—or faith—to believe that He certainly *could* sell our house in a day if He so desired.

That Sunday morning, I went forward to the altar for prayer after the service, again to solicit prayer for our one-day sale. It seemed ironic that even as the "shepherd" anointed me with oil and proceeded to pray for me, he seemed not to pray believing God would, but only that my faith would continue to be strong!

At 1:00 P.M. many visitors streamed through our doors, but by 3:00 P.M. not *one* person had placed a bid on the house or expressed a serious interest in buying it. At that point, my husband went to the car wash, and my son "bailed" on me and went to Grandpa and Grandma's down the street!

Alone in my family room, I looked up at God, then down at my Bible, and sincerely asked, "Did I hear You wrong, or did You tell me that You would sell my house in a day?" Opening to Isaiah, I read, verse after verse, hoping for a glimpse or sign of His word to me. Then Isaiah 51:5 stood out on the page as if it were one-fourth inch higher than all the other verses: "My righteousness draws near speedily, my salvation is on the way."

"That's it," I said aloud, closing my Bible. He did tell me. And whoever is going to buy this house is on the way!

The doorbell rang and a prospective couple entered. Before I could even start showing them the house, another couple entered the front door. Fortunately, my husband had returned and was coming in the door behind them.

One hour earlier that couple had been headed south on the highway. Picking up the newspaper, they ran across our open house ad and made an unplanned turnaround. By five o'clock that afternoon the sale by owner papers were signed, and the rest is history!

To us, the sale of our house in one day was a miracle! To our family and friends who witnessed the prompt sale of our house, it was a miracle! From that experience, I didn't learn to pray for miracles, I learned that it is okay to ask of God. I can't say this any stronger: God invites us to ask. He is willing to answer. He calls us to "approach the throne of grace with confidence, so that we may receive mercy and find grace to help us in our time of need" (Heb. 4:16).

Have you ever witnessed or experienced a miracle or an unexplainable answer to prayer?

☐ Yes   ☐ No

Do you believe this was a result of prayer?

☐ Yes   ☐ No

Do you believe that God can work miracles?

☐ Yes   ☐ No

Are you willing to ask God to work a miracle?

☐ Yes   ☐ No

In what area of your life do you most need God's advice, intervention, or help?

_____

_____

_____

_____

Will you accept the answer or advice that He gives you? Explain.

_____

_____

_____

_____

To some people, a miracle would be classified as the healing of a tumor that disappeared without explanation. I would consider the healing of a tumor and the sale of a house in one day both as occurrences where God has divinely intervened.

Perhaps one of the most difficult prayers Christians will pray is to ask God to heal someone. Prayer for healing seems harder to understand than anything that we can try to understand about God.

Many ask the same questions:

• Does God heal today as He did in the New Testament?
• Is He reluctant to heal?
• Can *we* do something to assure we will be healed?

I have been on both sides of the healing prayer. I have asked God for healing from alcoholism and received it. And I have asked God for a healing for a friend with cancer and not received what we had asked of Him. Based on all of the Scriptures I have read about asking God, I am left with one assessment: God is sovereign. We are free, even encouraged, to ask Him to intervene in our lives, but He still holds the answer.

I truly believe that God wants us to ask anything of Him at any time. In Philippians 4:6, we are encouraged to pray about everything, and in 1 Peter 5:7, we are exhorted to cast our anxieties upon Him because He cares for us! When it comes to talking to God, we are encouraged to include everything in our prayers. He *wants* us to come to Him with our concerns over these things:

- Finances
- Trials
- Children's needs and problems
- Relationships
- Personality struggles
- Housing needs
- Goals and dreams
- Emotional pain
- Insecurities

A receiving or an asking prayer is just that—it is a request. When we ask God with deep desire and passion, with hope and faith and perseverance, with a clean heart and pure motives, we have done our part. If we have been diligent to pray, then we can believe that God's answer will come in His timing in His way, and it will not be the wrong answer.

I am forever referring to O. Hallesby's quote: "When God says 'yes,' it is because He loves us. When God says 'no,' it is because He loves us." If we were to live as if we truly believed the words of that quote, then our faith could take on a new strength. We would no longer need to battle our emotions or resign to a belief that our prayers are meaningless, unimportant, powerless, or unnecessary. When we believe that God's yes or no is the most appropriate, even His absolute best response—given all that He knows—we will be motivated to pray with confidence, fervency, and conviction. Approaching God can then be considered our privilege—our incredible opportunity—to have an open conversation with the King of all kings.

Share a time that you received a "no" answer to prayer and only later could understand that it was the best answer at that time.

_____

_____

_____

_____

_____

_____

_____

_____

_____

_____

_____

HAVING FAITH IN THE GOD WE ASK

When we candidly discuss the injustices of our lives with God, we must be able to trust that we have a just God as our arbitrator. When we cry out in pain to God, we must believe that we have the ear of One who has suffered from loss (the Father) as well as from pain and sacrifice and betrayal (the Son). When we request, ask, and petition for a reversal, an answer, an exception—as did Moses and Abraham—we must understand that we are not second-guessing or "tipping" God over to our side. Instead, we are appealing for God's absolute discernment for us and favor on us. When we pray, we must see ourselves as His beloved children, whom He walks with, lives in, and uses to bring glory to His name through these answered prayers.

At this time, write a note to God in the space provided, sharing any reservations or misconceptions that you have about asking (or receiving) prayer.

_____

_____

_____

_____

_____

_____

_____

When God Says No

Why would a loving Father withhold a "yes" answer from His favored child? It would make sense only if He knew the future and understood the consequences of His answer from an all-encompassing, eternal viewpoint. If a trusted Father chose to answer no, one would have reason to believe that the Father had proceeded with His answer based on His love for that child, not out of reluctance or power or anger.

Daily conversations with God can, will, and should become much more than just asking prayers. As within any intimate relationship, talking is the time and place to pour out

hopes and dreams,

   hurts and disappointments,

      physical and emotional pains, and

         even weaknesses and personal failures to God.

If we nurture and cultivate our relationship with God, prayer will become the place where miracles are born, power is released, and changes occur.

Talking honestly and regularly, daily, even moment by moment to God about those concerns makes

the waiting,

   the watching,

      the holding on,

         the persevering, and

            the revising of our expectations

manageable! Then when He answers, we are off on a dynamic (sometimes Indiana Jones–type) adventure.

What is an area of your life right now that you would like to ask God to intervene in, change, or redesign? It might be maintaining a relationship, purchasing a home, moving to a new location, changing jobs or occupations, getting pregnant, going to college, or getting married.

Openly discuss, in written prayer to God, the most significant area of need that you have right now.

_____

_____

_____

_____

_____

_____

_____

_____

_____

_____

_____

_____

_____

_____

_____

_____

_____

_____

_____

_____

Has this chapter helped change your perspective of receiving or asking in prayer? If so, in what way?

_____

_____

_____

_____

_____

_____

If you consider the purpose of asking or receiving prayers as the way to end all discomfort or injustice in your life, then you'll never find true satisfaction in prayer. If you are willing to consider prayer as the place where life truly unfolds, where you are heard, where dreams and ideas are born, where troubles are dealt with, understood, and faced, you will be drawn to spending time with God in prayer, unafraid to ask of Him, unafraid of His answers.

Up to this point in your life, what has been your *purpose* in prayer?

_____

_____

_____

_____

_____

Prayer, as described in the words of Ros Rinker, is "a conversation between two people who love each other." When we truly believe, are convinced, and are confident that the Father loves us, we are able to accept a "no" answer as well as a "yes" answer to our requests.

CHAPTER 11

REVEALING PRAYER

Consider this: James is speaking to you about prayer. He says, "If any of you lacks wisdom, he should ask God, who gives generously to all without finding fault, and it will be given to him" (James 1:5). James was encouraging the twelve tribes that were scattered among the nations to ask God to reveal His will to them, especially if they were uncertain of His will or lacking in wisdom. He told them that it did not make God angry or frustrated with them when they asked Him for help or answers. James encouraged them—and us—to *ask God!*

Is there an area in your life in which you feel uncertain of God's will or need His wisdom in handling a problem? Explain the situation in the space provided.

_____

_____

_____

_____

_____

_____

_____

James 1:5 is a guideline for me when I don't know how to pray. Often, I know what I want, but this revealing prayer principle is my method of finding out what God wants for or of me. I regularly ask God,

"What are Your will and plan for me in this situation?"

"Where would You have me to go?"

"What would You have me to do, Lord?"

James 1:5 has become the standard verse for reminding me that when I don't know how or what to pray, I can ask God, "What is Your will?" Perhaps we don't ask God for advice—most often—because more than anything else we are afraid of His answer.

How would our lives be different if we were to make it our habit, pattern, and prerequisite *before* buying something, moving, changing jobs, or taking a big step to say to the Lord, "I'm lacking wisdom. I'm not sure what I should do here. Would You please show me what to do?" From all that I've read and experienced about prayer, I believe God wants us to ask Him for advice and He desires to give us an answer or to show us the way to go.

My most fun illustration of a revealing prayer happened during a time when I was hoping to improve my speaking skills. While living in Cleveland, Ohio, I attended the beginning level C.L.A.S.S. (Christian Leaders and Speakers Seminars) that was held in Columbus, Ohio. It was there that I heard of ADVANCED C.L.A.S.S., which was taught by Florence and Fred Littauer and held in southern California. While at C.L.A.S.S., I felt as if attending a speaker's training event was *just the beginning* of something that God had for me to do. My heart burned with desire to go to ADVANCED C.L.A.S.S., where attendees would be taught advanced techniques in public speaking. I had only three small problems: (1) It was being held in southern California, (2) I would have to clear it with Roger, my husband, and (3) I would have to find the money in our checkbook. Being on a parachurch ministry staff, we didn't have a monthly income that provided for gallivanting across the country, especially without advance notice or planning. Nonetheless, I was convinced that God wanted me to go.

Not very carefully, but very enthusiastically, I told Roger, "God wants me to go to ADVANCED C.L.A.S.S. next month in southern California." But Roger said, "Becky, I give an inch and you take a mile."

"But, Rog, I believe God wants me to go!" He didn't budge. I prayed continuously about it, my yearnings only growing deeper. Then one night in bed, I asked Roger to reconsider. I said, "Dear, what would it take for you to believe God wants me to go to ADVANCED C.L.A.S.S.?" Without much delay, Roger replied, "He'd have to pay your way."

Roger didn't make things very easy for me, but I continued to pray fervently and read my Bible. I daily read verses that encouraged me rather than discouraged me about attending ADVANCED C.L.A.S.S. So I continued to ask God to allow me to go to California and to *please* pay my way!

Thirteen days later, while having my quiet time, I had the distinct thought, *Today is the day you'll know!* I actually looked up into the sky and said aloud, "Did You say that, or did I say that?" Matter-of-factly, I decided God must be telling me "today" He would show us His will. I looked for His answer everywhere—in both my mailboxes and in every phone call. By eight o'clock that evening I walked past the telephone and whispered, "Okay. I thought I'd know today. Did I listen wrong? Did You tell me I'd know today, or was I hearing things?"

At 8:30, the phone rang. It was Fred Littauer, calling from southern California. He said we'd not met, but he had a note that I was interested in ADVANCED C.L.A.S.S. How could he help?

Little did he know I needed a lot of help—to the tune of about five hundred dollars. Without letting him know my dilemma, I asked about any payment plans or options for attending the seminar. He suggested using a credit card or prepaying in full. With that, the case was closed, but we continued to chat regarding current speaking and writing opportunities. As I hung up the phone, I thought to myself, *Well, I guess I did find out today!*

Ten minutes later the telephone rang. "Becky, this is Fred Littauer again. God has impressed upon my heart to offer you a scholarship to ADVANCED C.L.A.S.S. this June in southern California." Much later I found out that there had never been such an offer before—or since! Boy, were there hootin' and hollerin' in the Tirabassi home that night!

In addition, because of the initial contacts I made with a woman at ADVANCED C.L.A.S.S. (later she became a dear friend), my husband and I heard of a job opening at her church, and one year later we were hired and moved to California to direct their youth ministry.

The principle of revealing prayer unleashed a freedom in my prayer life to ask God and not be afraid that He would rebuke or scold me for wanting to know His will. (Note: The next step, how I respond to His direction, often takes much more faith than does the asking!)

How free do you feel to ask God for things? (Check one.)
- ☐ I can ask Him anything; no problem.
- ☐ I am comfortable asking Him for some things.
- ☐ I am a little bit uncomfortable asking Him for things.
- ☐ I feel as if I can't or shouldn't ask Him anything.

Recently when my husband, Roger, was considering a job change, he interviewed for three part-time positions, each in a different area of the country. All three were exciting opportunities, but one offered the best pay, the best location, and the least amount of change for our family. Selfishly, we would have chosen "the best" one in a heartbeat, but Roger wanted to be sure that we made our choice based on God's will for our lives, not on what we thought offered us "the best."

It was not a new concept to ask God to show us His will, but it was more difficult to carry out when the opportunities varied so much. So we prayed, "Lord, we know which job we would take, but we want You to show us Your will. Please close two doors and leave the one door open that You would have us to walk through." He did just that! Within two days, the financing and availability of two of the job opportunities completely changed. The one job (and door) that was left open was the one we would have chosen. It was the only one left to take.

Revealing prayer is a principle for any prayer request but is most appropriate when you are uncertain of God's will and truly "lack wisdom."

Proverbs 2 proclaims,

> And if you call out for insight
>   and cry aloud for understanding,
> and if you look for it as for silver
>   and search for it as for hidden treasure,
> then you will understand the fear of the LORD
>   and find the knowledge of God.
> For the LORD gives wisdom,
>   and from his mouth come knowledge and
>   understanding.
> He holds victory in store for the upright,
>   he is a shield to those whose walk is blameless,
> for he guards the course of the just
>   and protects the way of his faithful ones.
> Then you will understand what is right and just
>   and fair—every good path (vv. 3–9).

Write a prayer in the space provided, either summarizing Proverbs 2:3–9 or asking God directly for the qualities listed in the verses.

_____

_____

_____

_____

_____

_____

_____

_____

_____

_____

_____

Call out, cry aloud, look for, and search for God's will, and you will find it! He will reveal His will to you without scolding you. Begin by asking.

CHAPTER 12

BELIEVING PRAYER

If you believe, you will receive whatever you ask for in prayer.—Matthew 21:22

What happens when your dreams are so big that they could be achieved only with and by God's intervention? In my research, I uncovered stories about a man named George Mueller. He has been a vivid example to me of a man who did what he believed God wanted him to do, even against the odds, circumstances, or lack of capital—and without asking people for help.

He was said to have been a believing pray-er. He would pray unceasingly for the physical needs of the orphans he fed, clothed, and housed in the late 1800s in England. Witnesses tell that even if there was no food to eat, he would sit the children down at the dining table to pray. After the prayer, a knock would come at the door, and there would be baskets of food left at the doorstep—enough to feed those sitting at the table!

It was said of George Mueller that he fed, housed, and clothed orphans *without asking people* for food, money, or housing, but by asking God in prayer—thousands of prayers in each day—to supply their very specific needs. He firmly believed that God's power would be released when he prayed *because* he was doing God's will, fulfilling God's call on his life, and marching onward in the dream God had put in his heart to do!

How does this story relate to you?
- ☐ It makes me excited to ask God to fill my needs.
- ☐ It makes me realize how powerful God truly is and how little credit I've been giving Him.
- ☐ It inspires me to begin to ask and trust in God to provide.
- ☐ It does not apply to my life.
- ☐ I don't believe the story.

In addition to being inspired by George Mueller's life, I've been challenged to become a believing pray-er. I have been convinced that if the principles of prayer that are in the Bible are taken seriously, they will cause anyone who practices them to become the beneficiary of them! In other words, believing prayer is not just for George Mueller.

Do you believe you could ever have such power in prayer?
- ☐ Yes   ☐ Maybe   ☐ No

Would you like to have your prayers answered as George Mueller's were?

☐ Yes   ☐ Maybe   ☐ No

What would it take for you to become a believing pray-er?

_____

_____

_____

_____

_____

My favorite illustration of a believing prayer—which has had a great effect on how I pray—is found in a story about George Mueller:

Norman Harrison in *His in a Life of Prayer* tells how Charles Inglis, while making the voyage to America a number of years ago, learned from the devout and godly captain of an experience which he had had but recently with George Mueller of Bristol. It seems that they had encountered a very dense fog. Because of it the captain had remained on the bridge continuously for 24 hours when Mr. Mueller came to him and said, "Captain I have come to tell you that I must be in Quebec on Saturday afternoon." When he was informed that it was impossible, he replied, "Very well, if the ship cannot take me, God will find some other way. I've never broken an engagement for 57 years. Let us go down to the chart room and pray." The captain continued the story thus. "I looked at that man of God and thought to myself, 'what lunatic asylum could that man have come from?' I never heard such a thing as this. 'Mr. Mueller,' I said, 'do you not know how dense the fog is?' 'No,' he replied, 'my eye is not on the density of the fog but on the Living God who controls every circumstance of my life.' He knelt down and prayed a simple prayer and when he finished I was going to pray but he put his hand on my shoulder and told me not to pray. 'Firstly,' he said, 'because you do not believe God will. And secondly, I believe God has. There is no need whatever for you to pray about it.' I looked at him and George Mueller said, 'Captain, I have known my Lord for 57 years and there has never been a single day that I have failed to get an audience with the King. Get up and open the door and you will find that the fog has gone.' I got up and indeed the fog was gone. George Mueller was in Quebec Saturday afternoon for his engagement. I learned from that man that if you know God and if you know His will for your life and circumstances seem impossible, pray believing that God will—and He will!"

What is your reaction to this story about George Mueller?

_____

_____

_____

_____

_____

_____

_____

Not daily or even weekly, but occasionally, I am motivated from within to take a bigger step of faith and believe that God is speaking to me, calling me, and prodding me to believe something will come to pass that might not seem possible based on the circumstances.

This story has been a reminder to me that when we are in a relationship with God on a daily basis, He just might orchestrate an event, in an out-of-the-ordinary way, that will bring Him glory and increase the faith of those around us.

This happened for me in 1994 when the Billy Graham Crusade was coming to Cleveland, my hometown. Though I was living in California, my husband and I had spent ten years working for Cleveland Youth For Christ. When the local Crusade committee offered my name as a guest testimony to the national Crusade committee, they admitted never hearing of me and were not too open to having an unknown person as an evening speaker.

Upon receiving their response, I had a very unusual reaction. In my heart and mind, it seemed that before all time, God could very well have planned that I would share my dramatic conversion to Christ in the very town that I had become a teenage alcoholic. I thought a lot about it and prayed regularly about it as well. The more I prayed, the more I became convinced that if God did have this for me, He would have to convince the established committee to take a risk on an unknown speaker. What initially seemed to be a huge obstacle eventually didn't seem to be a very big thing to overcome if God wanted it to be done!

So I continued to pray. The more I prayed about it, the more I began to believe that God was going to have me speak at the Northeastern Ohio Billy Graham Crusade in June of 1994—the committee just hadn't decided to invite me yet!

A close friend of mine thought that I was so confident, he was afraid I was going to be disappointed. But my prayers didn't focus on begging God to have them invite me. I focused my prayers to say, "If this is Your very plan for me, Lord, please put it on their hearts to invite me, though they don't know me."

With those whom I asked to pray with and for me, I didn't tell them that God had told me I would speak there; I told them that I believed God could have this planned for me before all time. I also informed them that I was daily encouraged in prayer and Bible reading rather than being given any checks in my spirit or red flags during my appointments with God. I felt God allowed me *to pray believing*.

Have you ever felt strongly that God was leading you toward a desire you've had?

☐ Yes   ☐ No   ☐ Maybe

If the answer is yes or maybe, describe the situation and your feelings. Share the outcome.

_____

_____

_____

_____

_____

_____

_____

_____

_____

About five months before the Crusade, the invitation came over the telephone: "Would you share your testimony on Thursday night of the Northeastern Ohio Billy Graham Crusade?" The invitation served as confirmation of what I had already come to believe in my heart—God had prepared for me before all time. On June 9, 1994, I spoke, eighteen years after my conversion to Christ, before forty-two thousand people, some of whom were my own unsaved family members and friends.

While waiting for the outcome of a believing prayer—in the midst of the circumstances around us that are out of our control—we can pray. There we will find, as did George Mueller, an audience with the King!

CHAPTER 13

INTERCEDING PRAYER

Since so many people have written about interceding or intercessory prayer, you might be asking, "Why should I read *another* chapter on such a well-covered subject?" My answer is this: "If intercessory prayer is *not* part of your daily devotional life, then you still have some reading to do!"

I have a number of reasons that I pray for others:

- I might be the only person praying for them (who believes that prayer makes a difference).
- My prayer might just be the prayer to break through the barrier.
- During prayer for the situation, I might receive insight or encouragement to share with those involved.
- If I were in great need of prayer, I would be extremely grateful to anyone who would take the time and make the effort to pray for me.

Can you think of additional reasons why you should intercede in prayer for others?

_____

_____

_____

_____

_____

In *My Partner Prayer Journal*, I have maintained a daily prayer list that has only grown. (One enduring quality of a prayer list is that it never seems to get shorter!) Though many, many prayers are answered and no longer need to be listed, when others know that you will pray for them, they will ask you to pray and your list grows again! God has a way of bringing people and situations to your attention that prompt you to pray. By investing in the lives of others through interceding prayer, you'll become convinced that prayer is an absolute power source for the believer. You'll also consider yourself foolish not to pray!

In addition to the sheer power released when you pray for someone, William Law said that "nothing makes us love a man so much as praying for him." I found this to be true, especially when praying for those I don't know. For instance, while praying for presidents I have voted for (Reagan and Bush during the 1980s), I often felt a sense of concern for their safety and asked God to give them godly discernment in making decisions. Though I never had the chance to meet them, I often thought that if I did, I would give them a great big hug. I had grown to love them through the many years of praying for them.

When I had the opportunity to pray for a president I didn't vote for, I also began to grow in concern for him, his family, and his spiritual life and to pray that God would give him discernment in making decisions. I can honestly say that anger and malice were never parts of my feelings toward that president. Prayer had developed a love in me for a fellowman whom God had allowed—in His sovereignty—to be our leader, the president of the United States.

Interceding prayer gives us a wonderful opportunity to take immediate action on behalf of people in the service, estranged family members, people with addictions, hurting teenagers, married couples who are struggling, and people we know are ill.

Prayer is not a passive, boring, worthless act. It is an aggressive, determined, persistent way to use a powerful resource that we, as believers, have been given.

Have you ever maintained an intercessory prayer list?

☐ Yes ☐ No

If your answer is yes, describe your experience.

_____
_____
_____
_____
_____
_____

My interceding prayer list begins with a "be" list. I ask God to help me each day to be all that I can to all those I influence or am in contact with so that His name would be glorified. By beginning my prayer list with prayer for myself, I am reminded daily that all I do and say reflects on the God I love. It is very important to me to never shame God's name. I am equally aware that if I pray for one hour a day, but have a reputation for hatred, lust, love for the things of this world, a foul mouth, or an insatiable appetite for something considered ungodly, my prayers will reap little and shed a poor light on God, doing harm rather than good for His name. Therefore, my prayer list begins with me—getting right with God, living right with others, checking my motives in prayer, and asking God to cleanse me of any sin.

Next, I pray for each member of my family—very specifically. I have prayed for my husband's job opportunities, teaching opportunities, health, and recreation. And I can honestly say that I feel that my prayers have been a part of the success he has experienced. In fact, I believe they were instrumental in directing him to his current position as a pastoral counselor, even to the office space he leases and the number of clients he sees. Prayer has increased the love and respect that I have toward my husband. What a great privilege I have had to pray daily for him! It has truly caused me to be highly invested in his future, decisions, joys, and sorrows.

The next page of my intercessory prayer list includes every aspect of my son Jacob's life. Once he began driving, his single page has grown to two pages in the REQUESTS section of *My Partner Prayer Journal.* For all of these years I have prayed for his wife, that she would be a godly young woman, loved and protected by her parents and by God. I told my son that I'm going to know his wife before he does! I tell him that she'll walk in our door someday, and I'll say, "I've been waiting for you!" When he asked if I knew who she was, I told him, "I'm not telling!" In addition, I pray for his relationships, spiritual growth, and character development. Because I have a very current prayer list for my son, I update it daily as new issues arise.

List the ways you would like to pray for your family.

_____

_____

_____

_____

_____

_____

_____

_____

_____

_____

_____

Charles Stanley's comment, "Don't pray about anything you wouldn't want God to do through you," has influenced my intercessory prayers. While praying for my son to read his Bible during his sixth-grade year, I realized that it was not Jake's desire for himself but my hope for him. Therefore, in considering this prayer request in light of Charles Stanley's advice, I began to read the Bible each morning to my son before he got out of bed. (I had a captive audience because he always lay in bed until the very last minute. Of course, I would read the Bible stories with a great deal of excitement and drama, and he would oblige me by listening attentively—though one eye was open and one eye was closed.)

After I have prayed for my immediate family, I begin to pray for my extended family, then friends, coworkers, neighbors, and even new acquaintances. I have a list of names of people who need specific healing for cancer, injuries, and addiction. Because I have prayed for so many years for so many different people, I am not naive enough to think that a prayer will be answered in my time frame. Perhaps I used to think that way, but through the years, I have grown to realize that prayer is my powerful resource to make requests of God, not tell Him what to do and when to do it.

For me, intercessory prayer has taken spontaneous prayer to the next level. It is in interceding prayer that I purpose to pray for someone regularly rather than haphazardly. It is where I believe I can help fight the battle. Interceding for another is a privilege and a responsibility. It requires discipline, passion, and time.

The REQUESTS section of *My Partner Prayer Journal* has given me the place to become disciplined and committed to intercessory prayer. I know myself very well. If I were to close my eyes and try to remember who to pray for, I would forget and probably begin to daydream. By having a list in front of me with the names of the missionaries I pray for and financially support, I am reminded to pray for them and send in their monthly support. By praying for my pastor, his wife, and children, I believe that I am being a responsible church member, actually making a difference in my church's welfare.

I prayed for more than five years for teenagers who were struggling with their faith during their college years, so I was exhilarated when they called and told me that they had been going to Bible study or had been called into youth ministry. I could see the value in those daily prayers that were invested on behalf of their lives.

Again and again, I am compelled to pray for people I encounter at the hair salon, on an airplane, or in a hotel. I pray for them in specific ways and have been able to see that these prayers have had an impact on the course of their lives.

Have you ever had an encounter with a stranger that you felt was an appointment from God?

_____

_____

_____

_____

_____

Are there any people you have met lately whom you could pray for?

_____

_____

_____

_____

In many of the New Testament letters, there is encouragement to intercede for others in prayer. In Philippians, Paul said, "I thank my God every time I remember you. In all my prayers for all of you, I always pray with joy because of your partnership in the gospel. . . . And this is my prayer: that your love may abound more and more in knowledge and depth of insight, so that you may be able to discern what is best and may be pure and blameless until the day of Christ" (1:3–5, 9–10).

In Ephesians, Paul prayed with these words:

I have not stopped giving thanks for you, remembering you in my prayers. I keep asking that the God of our Lord Jesus Christ, the glorious Father, may give you the Spirit of wisdom and revelation, so that you may know him better. I pray also that the eyes of your heart may be enlightened in order that you may know the hope to which he has called you, the riches of his glorious inheritance in the saints, and his incomparably great power for us who believe (1:16–19).

Paul asked the Ephesians to pray for him: "Pray also for me, that whenever I open my mouth, words may be given me so that I will fearlessly make known the mystery of the gospel, for which I am an ambassador in chains" (6:19–20). In 3 John, John wrote to his dear friend Gaius, saying, "I pray that you may enjoy good health and that all may go well with you" (v. 2). Whether praying for leaders, family members, or friends, for their health or their safety, the purpose of intercessory prayer is to lift up, go between, and go before those in need with powerful and effective prayers.

If you are not an intercessory pray-er, now might be a perfect time to ask yourself, Why not? Andrew Murray gave us one good reason to ponder: "The devil's greatest tool is to keep the believer from praying!" Could it be that your laziness or ignorance about the power of prayer has kept you from making a difference in the lives of those around you through prayer?

Summarize any verses from those mentioned that you feel might be speaking to you today.

_____

_____

_____

_____

_____

_____

_____

_____

_____

_____

I am confident that prayer is available to the believer at any given time of any day for any problem whatsoever. There is no locked door, no busy signal, no unanswered or unreturned phone calls in the prayer line. We are always connected, always on-line. Is it time for you to become an intercessor?

CHAPTER 14

AGREEING PRAYER

I say to you that if two of you agree on earth concerning anything that they ask, it will be done for them by My Father in heaven. For where two or three are gathered together in My name, I am there in the midst of them.—Matthew 18:19–20 NKJV

I have a prayer partner who lives 2,500 miles away from me. When we first became prayer partners, we lived only about 45 miles apart. In reality, both distances were far enough to cause us to pray over the telephone for the past eleven years.

Early in my prayer discovery, God used our friendship and prayer partnership to teach about the principle of agreeing prayer. But prior to my discovery of prayer in February of 1984, I always felt that prayer partners and prayer rooms were for older people or for prayer warriors. None of those titles appealed to me, so I avoided them.

Fill in the blanks with five adjectives that come to your mind when you think of prayer partners, prayer rooms, prayer meetings, and prayer warriors.

————————, ————————, ————————, ————————,

————————

We came together as prayer partners naturally. Immediately following my decision to pray for one hour a day, Kinney was the first friend I challenged to join me in my prayer hour. Our friendship was relatively new at that time because her husband was recently named to the board of directors of Cleveland Youth For Christ and my husband was the executive director of Cleveland Youth For Christ. We were about the same age (thirty years old), and both had been Christians for only eight years.

Not coincidentally as my enthusiasm and commitment bubbled over afresh about prayer, her enthusiasm for prayer grew. As I barraged her with my exciting discoveries about prayer and as the determination to write my prayers became a discipline in my life, she was the first to hear about them. She also was the local friend who kept me accountable to my hour prayer commitment.

The answers to prayer that we witnessed seemed so awesome, even miraculous, that we found ourselves agreeing more and more often in prayer. We would even meet in parking lots, halfway between our homes, to pray!

By the end of that year, Kinney and I grew closer as friends, sharing our joys and struggles. During that first year, Kinney told me she was unable to have children. In October, Kinney and I attended a women's retreat together. It seemed a timely lift to her spirits because a recent adoption attempt had failed very late in the procedure, causing her much emotional pain.

If Kinney and I had been close friends one year earlier, we probably wouldn't have felt that strongly about the power of prayer. But for the previous eight months, we had been on a wild jungle safari, uncovering new truths about prayer as two young thirty-year-olds finally getting serious about the serious things of God. Not having other options or answers, we impulsively decided to visit the prayer room.

As we walked into the empty room, I mused that it was a first-ever visit to a prayer room in my entire life. Compelled to kneel by two chairs, we prayed for almost forty-five minutes over the situation at hand: the inability to have children (though every conceivable test and operation had been tried), a terribly disappointing, incomplete adoption, and now, perhaps even worse, a loss of hope. We prayed. We cried and tremblingly asked God for a baby, allowing Matthew 18:19 to serve as a reminder "that if two of you agree on earth concerning anything that they ask, it will be done for them by My Father in heaven" (NKJV).

That night, during a concert, a woman neither of us knew tapped Kinney on the shoulder and said, "I understand you are looking for a baby." We slowly looked at each other in awe and amazement! The incredible account of the next six weeks included an interview, more prayer, lots of applications, renewed hope, and a beautiful baby girl named Ginny! The story of Kinney's Ginny is perhaps the most dramatic account of agreeing prayer that has occurred in my life, but on a weekly basis it has become a practice to sit with family, friends, and staff members at spontaneous and planned moments and lift great and small needs up to God, agreeing with them in Jesus' name and leaving the incredible results up to Him.

Have you ever participated in an agreeing prayer that resulted in a powerful answer, like the one Kinney received? If so, describe your experience in the space provided. If not, write down a few reasons why you think you have not experienced this type of prayer or answer to prayer.

_____

_____

_____

_____

_____

_____

_____

_____

_____

_____

The following illustration has been distributed nationwide by evangelism and discipleship organizations, such as AD2000, to be shared with any who would like to make agreeing prayer a significant part of their Christian walk.

PRAYER TRIPLETS

What is a prayer triplet? It is a way to win other people to Christ. You link up with two Christians and pray together regularly for the salvation of nine friends or relatives who do not know Jesus personally and a country where Jesus is not known. Then rejoice as you see Matthew 18:19–20 fulfilled.

Here are the instructions:

Choose two Christian friends or relatives to make your triplet.

Each of you choose the names of three people who do not know Jesus as their personal Savior and Lord. Choose a country where Jesus' name is not now known or is rare.

Agree on a time to meet once a week to pray together for your nine. Just fifteen minutes in your home, at work, or at school, before or after a meeting, is all it takes.

Pray together for the nine people by name to accept Christ as their personal Savior and Lord, including their personal needs and frailties. Also pray for your country.

As much as possible, as God leads, involve yourself with your three in a friendly way. Pray for each other as you seek to do this.

When your friends become Christians, continue to pray for them, even if your triplet takes on other names to pray for.

If possible, incorporate them into your church, Bible study, and/or fellowship after they accept Jesus.

My prayer partners are

1. _____

2. _____

Their three names for us to pray for:

1. _____
2. _____
3. _____

1. _____
2. _____
3. _____

The people I've asked prayer for:

1. _____
2. _____
3. _____

Our unreached people group:

_____
_____

E. M. Bounds's famous exhortation, "Much prayer, much power. Little prayer, little power. No prayer, no power," has often prompted me to enlist others in a prayer request. Often a person will share a need or a situation that is currently unfolding and will request my prayer. I have tried to make it my habit to stop *right then and there* to agree with the person in prayer, believing that the more prayer offered for a situation, the more power is released!

From small to large agreeing prayers, God continually shows us that He is listening and is faithful. No matter the size or significance of the prayer request, I believe our prayers are important to Him. From the lost wallet to the potential job opening, from the mending of a relationship to prayer for financial rescue, agreeing prayer becomes a faith-building experience for those who are involved in it.

Praying with others for God's intervention creates excitement and motivation to keep on agreeing in prayer! I encourage you not only at prayer meetings but with your friends, during recreation times, at planning meetings, or on family vacations to make time for agreeing prayer.

In the space provided, list the names of as many relatives, friends, or acquaintances you can think of who might be possible prayer partners for you. Ask God to show you ones He would like you to spend time praying with.

_____

_____

_____

_____

_____

_____

_____

_____

_____

_____

_____

_____

_____

_____

_____

_____

_____

CHAPTER 15

PERSEVERING PRAYER

Then Jesus told his disciples a parable to show them that they should always pray and not give up.—Luke 18:1, emphasis added

Between Andrew Murray, George Mueller, R. A. Torrey, and Wesley Duewel, I am hard-pressed to tell you which man has been a greater mentor in my life when it comes to prayer. Having read dozens of their books on prayer, I find that a recurring theme is the principle of persevering prayer.

In my prayer life, perseverance has proven to bring rewards, but it has also been painful and sometimes difficult to understand. I don't say this to sound threatening; I just want to be truthful. If you are serious about prayer, this principle will undoubtedly weave itself through your prayer life, whether you like it or not!

Persevering prayer, as Jesus explained it to His disciples in the parable of Luke 18, is learning to pray and not give up. If you haven't yet found the desire to persevere in prayer, you *will* the first time you pray for someone who is in great need or for something that you feel passionately about.

In the classic book *The Power of Prayer*, R. A. Torrey spoke of persevering in prayer for unsaved children in this way:

> Oh, mothers and fathers, it is your privilege to lead every one of your children to the Savior. But it costs something to have them saved. It takes much time alone with God, to be much in prayer. It costs also your making those sacrifices, and straightening out those things in your life that are wrong; it costs fulfilling the conditions of prevailing prayer. And if any of you have unsaved children, get alone with God and ask Him to show you what it is in your own life that is responsible for the present condition of your children, and straighten it out at once and then get down alone before God and hold on to Him in earnest prayer for the definite conversion of each one of your children. Do not rest until, by prayer and by your putting forth every effort, you know beyond question that every one of your children is definitely and positively converted and born again. Are you a Sunday school teacher? Do you wish to see every one of your Sunday school scholars converted? That is primarily your duty as a Sunday school teacher. You are not merely to teach Bible geography and Bible history, or even Bible doctrine, but to get the scholars in your class one and all saved. Do you want power from on high to enable you to save them? Ask God for it.

Make a list of the top five prayer requests in your life that remain unanswered.

_____
_____
_____
_____
_____
_____
_____
_____
_____

In the space provided, record your reaction to R. A. Torrey's quote.

_____
_____
_____
_____
_____
_____
_____
_____
_____
_____
_____

In Wesley Duewel's book, *Mighty Prevailing Prayer*, he asks the reader, "Are you longing for power in prayer, the ability to get urgent and needed answers? Do you feel deeply tested at times by the unexplained delay in answers to your prayers? Are you longing for the secret to answered prayer?" He answers these questions only as a man who has practiced perseverance in prayer can exhort, "Prevailing prayer is prayer that obtains the answer sought. It overcomes delay, opposition, and unfavorable circumstances. It often involves the Spirit's guidance in how you pray and His deepening of your desire for the answer to prayer. It involves His specially empowering your prayer and strengthening your faith until you receive the answer from God."

Much of Andrew Murray's teaching about prayer overrides and undoes teaching about prayer that says we needn't offer up a prayer more than once. Instead, he exhorts us to pray as Jesus taught in Luke 18, with tenacity, boldness, and persistence that plead for mercy and justice. Andrew Murray, having written much about prayer, said, "The secret of persevering prayer was patience and faith."

George Mueller was ready to lead the way for anyone willing to persevere in prayer. It was said of him that prayer was "the cornerstone with which his life's work was built." It drove him forward, led him through difficulties and impossibilities, and fueled him with a faith to believe what he could not see. And though he waited up to twenty-nine years for certain prayer requests to be answered, he never gave up on God or in the practice of prayer.

All of these men have provided me with examples of why I should persevere in prayer, when I should persevere in prayer, and that I should persevere in prayer. Along with the Word of God, the words of these giants for God absolutely give me courage and confidence to persevere in prayer.

A most enduring example of persevering prayer was for the many Campus Life students that I prayed for during their four years of college, after they left my high school ministry. I prayed long, hard, and often that they would get right with God. And one by one, God has brought most of them back into my life to tell me that they have overcome their addictions, gone into ministry, are happily married, or are getting married and would like me to attend their wedding!

Another nineteen-year-long prayer request was for my high school friends. Back in 1976, they were just not interested in my conversion to Christ. By 1995, almost all of my dearest friends have come to know the Lord!

Do any people in your life need persevering prayer? List them in the space provided.

_____

_____

_____

_____

_____

_____

_____

_____

Persevering prayer is spiritual, taxing work that if not practiced will keep many of us from seeing the fruit of answered prayer. It takes a serious amount of time and attention to persevere in prayer, but it is attainable. Persevering in prayer, we will become like those described by Leonard Ravenhill, "Men who got unusual answers to prayer because they were unusual in prayer!"

Complete the following sentence with the phrase that best describes you:

Persevering prayer is
- ☐ something I practice each and every day.
- ☐ something I've never heard of before.
- ☐ a discipline I'm not yet ready for.
- ☐ a type of prayer I've never tried, but I'm excited to try now.
- ☐ something I'm still a bit (or a lot) skeptical about.

Be encouraged to persevere in prayer until God—in His mercy—answers you!

PART FIVE

A Deeper Walk

CHAPTER 16

THE BLESSINGS AND BENEFITS OF PRAYER

The closest I have come to feeling like a disciple of the Lord is when I spend time talking, laughing, crying, complaining, pleading with God, listening to Him, then allowing Him to correct, comfort, exhort, and direct me. Through my daily appointments with the King, I have grown to know, love, respect, and even willingly obey Him. I firmly believe that I could have *never* imagined or experienced these blessings had I not decided to pray an hour a day.

If I told you that my goal when I began to pray an hour a day was to become a holy, godly woman, that would not be honest. The truth behind my prayer commitment was that

I was

      emotionally insecure,

            humiliated in my laziness after God, and

                  disillusioned with my progress as a Christian.

I wasn't sure what I was looking for or getting into when I decided to make prayer a daily priority in my life, but I knew that I wanted and needed more excitement—even *feeling*—in my relationship with God.

What led you to pick up or purchase this workbook? What did you hope to accomplish in your prayer life by going through it? Explain.

When I was a new convert (or follower) of Jesus, I was expectant that God would answer my prayers. I kept a Bible with me at all times, certain that if I had a concern or question, I would find the answer in my Bible. And I was unashamed and open with strangers, family members, and coworkers about my faith in the Lord Jesus Christ.

But as years went by and I "matured" in the Lord (entering ministry, getting married, having a child), my prayer life suffered the most. My conversations with God lasted rarely more than a few minutes. They were always late at night, breathed from exhausted lips, and brought forth from a tired mind. My anemic devotional experience was what I longed to change. I was envious of my baby Christian days. My spiritual life was characterized by a constant hunger for fellowship with the Lord *because I needed Him and wanted His input into every aspect of my life,* not because I felt I had a duty or an obligation to carry out. Though I didn't know how to get back to that passion for God, I knew it was missing.

Is your situation similar to what the author described?

☐ Yes   ☐ No   ☐ Not sure

Explain why or why not.

_____

_____

_____

_____

_____

_____

_____

THE PASSION REVIVED

When I made the decision to pray for one hour a day, I found what I was looking for and much more. The benefits and blessings that have resulted from my February 1984 prayer commitment have been so abundant that I often echo the words of Psalm 40:5,

Many, O LORD my God,
    are the wonders you have done.
The things you planned for us
    no one can recount to you;
were I to speak and tell of them,
    they would be too many to declare.

Initially, we are greatly excited when we
    see answers to prayer,
        experience immediate personality changes, or
            watch long-awaited doors begin to open
as a result of concerted prayer. But there is more. A deeper
walk with God will result after hours and years of spending
time with God. It looks like this:

☐ Prayer fuels faith, prompting us to dream and hope
and risk.

☐ Prayer woos us to the Word by our need to hear God's
response to our requests.

☐ Prayer teaches trust in God through waiting upon His
timing.

☐ Prayer reveals God's plan and our purpose for the present and the future.

☐ Prayer releases God's power to live and walk in the
supernatural realm of the Holy Spirit.

☐ Prayer unleashes love for God—emotional, real, and
all-consuming.

From the above list, check one that you feel you most experience, and underline one that you most need in your life today.

THE PRIVILEGE
OF PRAYER

Though I am not an ordained pastor, a church staff member, a seminary graduate, or a member of a certain denomination, I've discovered that the privilege and power of prayer are available to all believers. No one is given special permission to pray because of sex, race, denomination, or degrees. Though many of us truly believe that prayer is a powerful resource and privilege, we still have to make a decision to pray. But when people finally arrive at the decision to make prayer a priority in their lives—whether it derives from conviction or desperation—they will see results and experience the blessings and benefits available to those who pray.

Who then, having thought through all the benefits and blessings of prayer, would consciously decide to eliminate, forget, or neglect time with God?

Let's walk on.

Check all the statements that best apply to you.
- ☐ Prayer is already a priority in my life.
- ☐ I am ready to make prayer a priority in my life.
- ☐ Prayer just isn't the priority it should be in my life.
- ☐ I'm still not ready to make prayer a priority in my life.

CHAPTER 17

PRAYER FUELS FAITH TO DREAM AND HOPE AND RISK

Perhaps one of the most compelling aspects of the spiritual life is to hold on to a faith that says, "My God sees, knows, hears, understands, and takes care of me." We vacillate somewhere between Hebrews 11:1 ("Now faith is being sure of what we hope for and certain of what we do not see") and Romans 8:28 ("All things work together for good to those who love God, to those who are the called according to His purpose" NKJV). Many of us wonder, waver, temporarily doubt, or are gripped with the fear that God might have forgotten us.

Describe the last time you felt that God might have forgotten you.

_____

_____

_____

_____

_____

_____

_____

If you have longed for a foolproof method of staying firm in your faith, you are not alone. Most of us wish we could be certain, better yet, *feel* certain that God was indeed watching over the following:

- People who make decisions that affect our lives (in government, on the job, and so on)
- Our children
- Our finances
- Our physical health (and the doctors treating us)
- Our past, present, and future

We tell ourselves that if we had a strong faith, we could walk through life much more confidently and faithfully and much less emotionally. Is there any hope for us?

I believe that prayer is meant to be our practical, tangible way to fuel our faith on a daily basis. Praying is like talking to the Architect of our lives. It is discussing the detailed blueprint of our future with the One who held the plan from before all time. In prayer, we realize that God is longing to divulge His plan for us.

Daily discussions with God, who is the author and perfecter of your faith, will put flesh and form to your dreams, giving you motivation to fulfill your life's purpose. Prayer is meant to give a calm assurance that God is listening, orchestrating, bringing about, and shaping the very details of your life. Just as a contractor would direct people building a structure one brick, then one wall at a time, God offers direction through daily prayer.

If you are not spending time with God on a regular basis, how can you expect to gain assurance that what you cannot see will happen? And if not from God, where will you otherwise gain your confidence and fuel your faith?

_____

_____

_____

_____

_____

_____

_____

_____

_____

_____

Faith comes from God. Based on written accounts of the men and women in the Old and New Testaments, faith has never been based on outer circumstances. Faith is—and always has been—based on the inner work of God in a person's

life where confidence and direction come into the heart and
mind through His Word and Holy Spirit.

In the space provided, write a personal definition of *faith*.

_____

_____

_____

_____

_____

_____

I have found that

- faith is taking a step in the direction toward what we
  believe God is calling, even asking, us to do.
- faith is obeying God in the unseen areas of our lives.
- faith cannot be mustered; it must be fueled by prayer
  and the Word.
- faith is the place where we stop relying on ourselves
  and begin trusting in the Lord.
- faith is a willingness to listen to—and obey—the string
  of thoughts that filter through our minds, directing us
  toward good and godly ways.
- faith is a whisper, a call, an intelligible, but usually not
  audible voice directing us to achieve something for the
  good of others.
- faith is pleasing God over anyone or anything else, no
  matter the outward circumstances (see Noah as an example).

Which one of these was closest to your definition of faith?

_____

_____

_____

_____

_____

Which ones have you experienced in your life?

_____

_____

_____

_____

_____

Which one would you like to experience more often?

_____

_____

_____

_____

Where does faith come from? Romans 10:17 states, "Faith comes by hearing, and hearing by the word of God" (NKJV). Through the Word, we hear God's voice. Thus faith comes when—and as—we hear God's voice.

When we pray—both talk and listen—we will hear God's voice. How? He will direct us to verses we have memorized, read, or heard in a sermon. He will speak to us in our daily planned Bible reading. He will speak to us through others who teach, speak, and refer us to the Word.

Faith comes when—and as—we connect with God. Prayer connects us to God. Prayer is a unique opportunity that we have been given to converse with the living God. But unlike human beings, God is never too busy, too far removed, or too judgmental to talk with us. I believe that God longs to talk to us, to connect with us.

In my experience, it is in and through prayer that God has released a myriad of ideas, goals, and dreams. They might have been new or lying dormant, but when no longer hindered by fears of failure or tripped up by stumbling blocks such as personal sin, shame, or guilt, I was empowered to risk and dream.

When you begin to spend time with God on a regular basis, your fears, besetting sins, shame from your past, and list of reasons why you "can't, didn't, or shouldn't" will begin to

pass away,

be resolved, or

be exposed

as excuses why you haven't reached your dreams or fulfilled your purpose in life. Prayer will wipe away those excuses and pry open the doors of faith, pushing you toward your dreams.

In the space provided, define what a *dream* is to you.

_____

_____

_____

_____

_____

_____

Have you felt in your lifetime that you've had a dream come true? Explain.

_____

_____

_____

_____

_____

_____

_____

Can we hinder or help our effectiveness in prayer?

_____

_____

_____

_____

_____

The more time we spend with God, the more we discover that we can hinder our prayers with unforgiveness, bitterness, or possibly even sin that we have been cherishing in our hearts (Ps. 66:18). These discoveries may not seem as exciting as the dusted-off dreams, but they are part of the process of achieving, seeing, and fulfilling those dreams.

On a scale of 1 to 10 (1 is way too much, 10 is not in the least), do you feel as if your prayer effectiveness is currently affected by holding on to negative feelings like those noted?

1   2   3   4   5   6   7   8   9   10

Now, list any fears, sins, doubts, or specific barriers that could be keeping you from reaching goals and dreams, or receiving an answer to prayer.

_____

_____

_____

_____

_____

_____

_____

_____

_____

_____

_____

_____

_____

_____

_____

_____

_____

_____

_____

STEPS TO A DREAM

Because a dream—any dream—is completed in steps until it is fulfilled, it might seem to drag on endlessly, stall, or even go in reverse! Prayer is the place to review your dreams and ask God to open doors—one day at a time. It is the vehicle that will bring perspective into your life.

I've heard that successful people list their goals, then diligently and daily review them. They even keep their goal list in a place where they will see it regularly (office, home, car, desk, or mirror).

Make a list of your dreams or goals that you have for your life in the next . . .

Ninety Days	One Year	Five Years
_____	_____	_____
_____	_____	_____
_____	_____	_____
_____	_____	_____
_____	_____	_____
_____	_____	_____
_____	_____	_____
_____	_____	_____
_____	_____	_____

(Later on, transfer this to your prayer list.)

I have carried this idea into my prayer life. A page in the REQUESTS section of *My Partner Prayer Journal* is strictly for my dreams. It is where I list the specific (and sometimes general) goals, hopes, and plans that I have. I have incorporated it into my daily P.A.R.T. in prayer *because I believe that God has put these dreams within me.*

For instance, my first aerobics video began on the DREAMS page of my request list. For many months, I asked,

"Lord, may I make a Christian aerobics video?" Two years later, I met the president of a company who agreed to produce my first video. Soon the video came off my DREAMS page of my prayer list and began a life of its own—on the NEW VIDEO page. My list grew to include the company's name and each decision we were facing at every step of the way. Because I was praying daily about the video, I also updated the list regularly as circumstances changed or the project needed revision.

The video project eventually grew to take more than four pages in the REQUESTS section of my notebook. Very specifically, I included every person's name who would have a part in its development, the names of the companies and key people involved, the music requirements, and the technical details (there were many). I even prayed about how the video would be perceived and succeed.

I am not a very patient person, but because I was talking to God about every detail, I was able to wait, trusting Him with the outcome. Often after daily prayer for the video, I was given ideas of people to call or other doors to knock on when certain details fell through a crack or a "no" answer left us in need. And through daily prayer for the project, I found the courage to persevere, the faith and confidence to keep hoping when things looked grim, and I gained determination not to give up.

Perhaps this is just where God would have us—helpless within our own strength, dependent on His deliverance. This balance in prayer allows Him to become strong in our weakness as well as receive the glory for the (often miraculous) answers to those prayers. Prayer fuels our faith to believe what we cannot see.

Again and again, the projects that I have completed have started as ideas in prayer. From there, the ideas turn into requests on my prayer list, and often, but not always, they become projects on my "to do" list.

THE IDEA FOR MY PARTNER PRAYER JOURNAL

As I mentioned earlier, even *My Partner Prayer Journal* was a result of a prayer. I didn't pray, asking God to give me a life work. My prayer was a prayer of desperation. I asked God to help me become more accountable and organized in my prayer life. I didn't ask Him to give me an idea for other people to use. I felt alone in my great—but genuine—desire to know God better.

But because I prayed in earnest, I believe that God heard my heart and gave me the idea to develop a prayer journal and to call it *My Partner*. When I say, "I *believe* that God gave me the idea," I didn't actually hear a voice, but I did get a thought and I began to write down the concept forming in my head. It came faster than I could develop it or think it through on my own.

Little did I know then that

- *My Partner Prayer Journal* would become the focus of my life and teaching.

- *My Partner Prayer Journal* would be a book that over two hundred thousand people would use to journal their prayers.
- I would develop a motivational speaking seminar where I would teach people to pray.
- I would start a company, My Partner Ministries, and make the first four thousand of these prayer journals in my home.

My Partner Prayer Journal has been one of my most exciting answers to prayer. Because of it, I have been able to enthusiastically share with others that written prayers give black-and-white proof of God's intervention, assistance, deliverance, and answers!

AND THE RISK GOES ON

Prayer doesn't stop with an idea or a list of to do's!

God brings others alongside to believe in your dream. With the prayer that birthed *My Partner Prayer Journal*, God brought along others to believe and share in the dream that He had put in my heart. A great faith booster occurs when, after you have persevered in prayer, people come to you to offer help, even if you haven't told anyone of your need. Often in the moments when you feel most rejected or discouraged, God brings His rescue, packaged in such a way to remind you that He is the designer, orchestrator, and giver of this dream. He uses others to encourage you and to fuel your faith.

Which of these words describes how you feel about praying for your dreams and goals?
- ☐ Encouraged: I will continue to be patient.
- ☐ Motivated: I am going to try it!
- ☐ Indifferent: I'm still not convinced.
- ☐ Excited: I can't wait to try it!
- ☐ Afraid: I don't want to be disappointed.

In *Let Prayer Change Your Life* (see pp. 128–29), I continue the saga of *My Partner Prayer Journal* with the story of how the person who had offered me the start-up capital to publish my first four thousand notebooks was the same person who told me about a large youth event, called CHIC (Covenant High Congress). While participating in CHIC in 1984, he felt that my prayer workshop would be an ideal addition to that quadrennial event. When he shared this exciting idea with me, I began to pray about it. I prayed for almost four years that I would be able to speak a CHIC.

As the details unfolded in an incredible way, I not only spoke at CHIC, but I was commissioned to write a devotional for all the students to receive at CHIC. (By the way, that little devotional had its birth in prayer two years before CHIC!)

What is the work or what are the dreams and desires that you believe God has given you to do that remain unfulfilled?

_____

_____

_____

_____

_____

_____

_____

_____

_____

_____

_____

When you pray, watch for small, medium, and large doors to open. These answers to prayer will be clear signs along the way of God's direction, goodness, faithfulness, and power being released on your behalf to fulfill the dreams He has put in your heart. Consider the occasions as the moments your adventure in prayer turn into an adventure in faith!

CHAPTER 18

PRAYER WOOS US TO THE WORD

Meant to sustain,
 inspire,
  motivate,
   increase faith,
    mature, and
     strengthen a believer,
the Word of God, when interwoven with prayer, serves as direction, guidance, conviction, comfort, a deterrent from sin, an escape, and a counselor. When our first response or our most compelling desire at any given time in any situation is to hunger for the advice found in God's Word, our relationship with God has the dynamics of a teacher-student, counselor-counselee, Lord and disciple.

In my devotional life, Bible reading is _____.

Fill in the blank with one of the following:
- A top priority
- Somewhat important
- Done whenever I can fit it in
- Seldom done
- Never done, but thought about!
- What devotional life?

Theophan the Recluse said if the Word and prayer were practiced simultaneously, they would produce certain feelings within the believer toward the Lord:

Do you wish to enter this Paradise as quickly as possible? Here, then, is what you must do. When you pray, do not end your prayer without having aroused in your heart some feeling towards God, whether it be reverence, or devotion, or thanksgiving, or glorification, or humility and contrition, or hope and trust. Also when after prayer you begin to read, do not finish reading without having felt in your heart the truth of what you read. These two feelings—the one inspired by prayer, the other by reading—mutually warm one another; and if you pay attention to yourself, they will keep you under their influence during the whole day. Take pains to practice these two methods exactly and you will see for yourself what will happen. God's spark, the ray of grace, will fall at last into your heart. There is no way in which you, yourself, can produce it: it comes forth direct from God.

Do you desire to have the kind of prayer life described?
☐ Yes   ☐ No   ☐ Not sure

Prayer draws us to the Word, and the two ignite to create a spark, even a flame, for the Lord. The Word in combination with prayer is meant to bring change to our circumstances, transform our minds, motivate our bodies to action, and cause us to make certain decisions, take deliberate steps, and stretch us to live and walk in the Spirit. But until Bible reading and prayer become our natural reaction when faced with a dilemma or a decision, we'll not experience the warmth described by Theophan or possess "the spark that allows God to confirm direction or grant peace amidst turmoil." If prayer is simply a last resort or call for help, or if we haphazardly search the Scriptures for guidance when everything else has failed, then we've missed God's true intent of how prayer and the Word are able to integrate moment by moment into our lives.

How quickly are you moved to search the Scriptures or to pray when faced with a dilemma? (Check one.)

☐ It is the first thing I do.

☐ It comes along second or third.

☐ I remember to do so only when reminded by someone else.

☐ It is always my last resort.

☐ I barely ever consult God's Word or pray to seek answers.

In *The Inner Life*, Andrew Murray proposes, "Prayer and the Word are inseparably linked together. Power in the use of either depends upon the presence of the other." He says, "The Word gives me guidance for prayer, telling me what God will do for me. It shows me the path of prayer, telling me how

God would have me come. It gives me the power for prayer, the courage to accept the assurance that I will be heard. And it brings me the answer to prayer, as it teaches what God will do for me."

Prayer and the Word of God unlock the doors that we long to see open. They should not be considered individual elements of a Christian's life; they should be thought of as two parts of one element. Faith will come—and grow—as we are reading and listening for God's voice in His Word to direct us. The Word will call and exhort us to prayer. Together, prayer and the Word, tried and tested, will increase our faith and release God's incredible power into our lives.

A deeper walk with God emerges when the Word is constantly blended with prayer in a believer's life. The phrase put your "hope in the word" is mentioned several times in Psalm 119. Because of that exhortation, it has become my practice to *hope* in the Word by asking God for a scriptural promise to hold on to or to hope in during times

when my endurance level is waning,

when I have been waiting long, or

when I have a big decision to make.

When I read a verse that gives a promise—His promise—to be my visible possession while waiting for the invisible to happen, I sense His intimacy, and I am given hope to sustain me in my waiting.

Open your Bible to the place where you've been reading lately, or if you haven't been reading lately, open to Psalm 1. Now read carefully until you see a verse that you feel could be a scriptural promise from God.

What is the verse? _____

_____

_____

_____

What does it mean to you? _____

_____

_____

_____

My Bible, especially the books of Isaiah and Psalms, is splashed with underlined verses, highlighted paragraphs, and dated references next to verses that were my hope during a court case, a broken relationship waiting to be mended, timely sermon texts, encouragement when I needed a lift, guidance for purchasing a new home or car or in accepting an invitation.

During your appointments with the King, your daily, regular Bible reading will weave itself with prayers to add to and confirm God's plan for your life. My rule of thumb has been to use the thoughts and impressions I receive in prayer and the verses I read in the Word together as confirmation to move me toward my dreams, help me make a decision, or cause me to pursue a course of action.

The practice of daily, regular Bible reading combined with two-way conversations with the Lord (prayer) develops an unwavering, lasting, firm faith.

CHAPTER 19

PRAYER TEACHES TRUST IN GOD'S TIMING

The more completely you cease being concerned about the time in which your prayers are to be answered, the more freedom you'll enjoy in your prayer life!—O. Hallesby

The most difficult aspect of prayer is waiting on God to answer us. How we wait on His timing says a lot about the depth of our trust in Him. No matter the request, a pattern develops when we pray that may unfold over days or weeks or even years.

First we pray . . .

then we wait . . .

then we receive an answer from the Lord.

The discipline of daily prayer is in itself a teacher, training us in how to wait on or trust in God's best. Over the course of the prayer journey, we will discover that much of what we ask of God is His will for us, but the timing is wrong! It is only later, when all the pieces fall into place, that we can ponder and appreciate the extra benefits of what more time and patient waiting allowed to unfold.

Looking back over your life, describe an event or series of events that were difficult to understand at the time, but now form an important piece of your life. How did God's hand work in your life?

_____

_____

_____

_____

_____

_____

_____

_____

Most recently, I was extremely disappointed over a miscommunication that seemed to undermine a relationship as well as throw a wrench in how I thought God was going to accomplish His will for me. In my heartache, and yes, anger, I could only pray. Next, I worked through forgiveness issues, eventually accepting the outcome of the ordeal not as devastating but as what God had allowed.

Intermittently, I fought off waves of remorse, frustration, and exasperation. Then oddly and unexpectedly, a new door with a very bright future opened. Because I was only recently free to open that door, I knocked, entered, and realized that the timing had never been better for such an opportunity.

Hanging in there through the discouraging moments and days by keeping honest communication lines open with God, I was finally able to see with new eyes. What I thought was a disaster was God allowing one door to close and a whole new door to open.

Do you identify with this story? In what way?

_____

_____

_____

_____

_____

_____

Though we may not receive the answer to our prayers as we had envisioned, our responsibility in prayer is to never stop waiting, trusting, praying, or expecting God to do "immeasurably more than all we could ask or imagine" in response to a request.

Accounts in the biographies of George Mueller, Hudson Taylor, Jim Elliot, Charles Finney, and Peter and Catherine Marshall detail tremendous stories of waiting and trusting and persevering in prayer. In some cases it was years before the answer to their specific prayer request was revealed to them by God. And so it will be in the lives of all believers who pray without giving up. They become the recipients of one or more of the following:

- Healing
- Job opening
- Miraculous serendipity by meeting someone special
- Financial blessing
- Long-awaited dream fulfilled at last

What do we find out about God at the end of a long-term wait? O. Hallesby reminds us that when He grants our prayers, it is because He loves us; when He does not, it is also because He loves us. We are to trust Him because He loves us.

On a scale of 1 to 10, rate how much you trust in God's love for you and in His will for your life (1 being with much reservation, 10 being without reservation).

1   2   3   4   5   6   7   8   9   10

Patience and perseverance in prayer come from waiting on God, not from begging Him. While waiting, I've found it helpful to ask God if I am praying rightly, or if I've been listening accurately. Trusting in His timing involves honestly and regularly evaluating my motives, examining whether they are impure or selfish, and being able to identify when my hopes might be centered on something other than God's will. If we trust in God's timing, we are willing to let Him alter or change our requests according to His plan.

Have you ever felt that you were persisting in prayer rather than waiting on God? How did it affect your daily life, your relationship with God, and your prayers?

_____

_____

_____

_____

_____

_____

_____

The phrases, comments, and clichés that remind us to just trust the Lord sound inspirational, but more often discourage us! Only through expectant waiting on God and His response can we develop an inner trust that God is in charge of the outcome, though the details are unseen.

CHAPTER 20

PRAYER REVEALS GOD'S PLAN AND OUR PURPOSE

This is the confidence we have in approaching God: that if we ask anything according to his will, he hears us. And if we know that he hears us—whatever we ask—we know that we have what we asked of him.
—1 John 5:14–15

After I made prayer a priority in my life, I read challenging verses on prayer, such as the opening Scripture, and my first thought was, *Do we really have whatever we ask of Him?* So often, rather than explore, deal with, or research the principles in the Word of God on our own, we'll ignore them or shy away from them because they seem too confusing or too far removed to apply to our lives.

In the space provided, write down the first few thoughts that come to your mind as you read 1 John 5:14–15.

_____

_____

_____

_____

_____

_____

Consider this: If God encourages us to ask, wouldn't it seem logical that He also plans to give us an answer? Most often we neglect to ask God for His plan and purpose in our lives, even though His Word clearly and repeatedly directs us to ask. At other times we might ask, but we neglect to listen to His response or are unwilling to obey His direction. Often we truly want to know God's will, but we get confused when the timing of His answer differs from our expectations. And if we succumb to our fears and deliberate within ourselves, as it says in James 1:5–6, we are "driven and tossed by the wind" (NKJV). Eventually, we might allow ourselves to become more influenced by our doubts than by God's willingness or goodness to provide for us. Exasperated, we either move impulsively ahead or repeatedly hesitate to pursue a specific course because we are not certain of God's plan and purpose for our lives.

Have you ever been afraid to ask God what His plan for your life is/was?

☐ Yes   ☐ No   ☐ Not sure

In the space provided, record your thoughts about why you are or have been afraid to ask about His plan for you.

_____

_____

_____

_____

_____

_____

_____

Abraham, Joseph, Moses, Joshua, Elizabeth, Mary, Sarah, David, Daniel, and Samuel (just to name a few) regularly asked God for His plan and will in their lives. Their whole lives illustrated that they were people who faced dilemmas and made decisions based on their conversations with God. They sought God for every detail of their lives, and He responded to them. They received direction, conviction, perseverance, details, confidence, and unusual power to overcome their enemies. Why would it be any different for the man or woman of God today?

Psalm 139:16 says that God has a plan for our lives:

All the days ordained for me
were written in your book
before one of them came to be.

Choose the segment that best completes the following sentence for you:

When I am faced with a dilemma, problem, or confusing situation, I

- ☐ run to the Lord in prayer.
- ☐ think about it until I feel I have chosen the best answer for me.
- ☐ waiver between options until I am totally confused.
- ☐ seek God's answer in prayer, but only after I've tried everything else.
- ☐ just go with whatever feels right at the time.

Frequently, people ask, "How do you know when God is saying no?" R. A. Torrey tells us to *pray through* until we see God's answer. He says, "We should never give up praying for it until we receive it or until God makes it very clear and very definite that it is not His will to give it." If I have waited long, receiving neither a yes nor a no, I will ask God to confirm the direction I am moving toward so that I will not unnecessarily move beyond, past, or ahead of Him. I continue to wait, recording my observations, even asking the Lord to show me if I am blind to my own selfishness, have impure motive, or have heard Him incorrectly.

Share two experiences from your life. First, write about a time when you felt that God showed you His purpose or plan for your life through an open door or a positive confirmation.

_____

_____

_____

_____

_____

_____

_____

Second, write about a time when you felt that God answered no to your request. Include your feelings, reactions, and any insight you might have today, looking back at the situation as it related to God's purpose and plan for your life.

_____

_____

_____

_____

_____

_____

Being in touch with God has definite implications for daily life. Communicating with God brings direction, peace, and contentment. Men and women connected with God are more apt to make decisions, plan, and understand the meaning and purpose for their lives because of God's influence on them. They do not chase the unknown; they fulfill their purpose in life, and they know it!

When I was a non-praying Christian, I was often anxious about what I knew *I wanted* to do, was perhaps even called to do, but lacked power, motivation, and courage to do. When

I began to pray each day, I spent quite a bit of time talking to God about His plan for my life. The more I prayed, the clearer it became. Soon, I knew confidently what I was to do and what steps I needed to take to get there.

I have pursued many of the ideas that I received in prayer and found all of them to be stepping-stones in fulfilling God's purpose in my life. From the very first step of His plan to the last step of God's purpose in my life, prayer continues to be the place to

sift through,

gain courage,

experience calm,

understand "no,"

express disappointment, and

find resolve!

Psalm 25:14 declares, "The LORD confides in those who fear him; / he makes his covenant known to them."

CHAPTER 21

PRAYER RELEASES GOD'S POWER

One of the most exciting results of prayer happens when God's power is released in our lives. When I began to teach people to write their prayers, I immediately received letters from many who agreed with my findings. They shared prayer stories and how incredible power was released in their lives or in the life of someone they knew or loved. They expressed the notion that God almost seemed to be waiting for them to come to Him in prayer so that He could answer them.

After having regular appointments with the King, most people experience that their dreams are dusted off, previous reasons for not praying are exposed as excuses, and long-standing stumbling blocks are removed as new doors swing wide open because of prayer.

Have you experienced the release of God's supernatural power in your life since you've been having regular appointments with God (or as you've been reading this workbook)? Record them in the space provided.

_____

_____

_____

_____

_____

_____

_____

_____

In the New International Version, James 5:16 reads, "The prayer of a righteous man is powerful and effective." In the New King James Version, it states, "The effective, fervent prayer of a righteous man avails much." That verse encourages, reminds, and exhorts a believer to pray because prayer is powerful.

Andrew Murray strongly believed that "the devil's greatest tool is to keep the believer from praying." Think about it! If your enemy knew you had a very effective and powerful weapon for winning battles, wouldn't it make sense for him to distract you from using it?

On the following list, check each reason that the enemy might use to keep you from praying:

☐ Busyness	☐ Overcommitment	☐ Laziness
☐ Stress	☐ Marital problems	☐ Sickness
☐ Work	☐ School	☐ Loneliness
☐ Hard times	☐ Fear	☐ Housekeeping

- ☐ Resentment
- ☐ A hard day
- ☐ Pride
- ☐ Doubt
- ☐ Unforeseen circumstances
- ☐ Tiredness
- ☐ Good times
- ☐ Children

I contend that a major reason people don't pray is that they have not experienced or witnessed the power of prayer for themselves. Power released because of prayer becomes more realistic when you've been part of a small group who is praying for an alcoholic and the alcoholic spontaneously quits drinking, having never entered a treatment center or received outside help. Then you become more prone to believe that prayer makes an absolute difference. Or when you've prayed for a job and are not qualified for it, but receive it against all odds, you will attribute that opportunity not to luck but to concerted prayer that moved God to move human hearts. Or as it happened for some Youth For Christ workers in the 1940s, after being refused entrance into the country of India, they went away to a room and used their resources, praying for twenty-four hours. By the end of their prayer vigil, they received a reversal of the original decision—and YFC is still in India fifty years later.

Because prayer is an incredible source of power for the believer, wouldn't it be unwise not to use it often—always as a first response rather than a last resort? Then why don't Christians pray more fervently? Certainly, we all face opposition, dilemmas, heartache, unresolved issues, disappointment, struggles, or illness. Don't we all have needs, whether great or small, for God's power to be released in our lives?

Can you name any areas of your life where you need God's power to be released?

_____

_____

_____

_____

_____

_____

_____

In the book of Acts, the experience of the early church was characterized by unexplainable healing and constant supernatural occurrences. R. A. Torrey, in *The Power of Prayer,* believed those things occurred because the early church was committed to prayer (Acts 2:42–44). Torrey promoted prayer as the vehicle that brings God's power into our work. He referred to Isaiah 40:31 as the Scripture describing how the believer receives power in prayer,

> Those who *wait* on the LORD
> Shall renew their strength;
> They shall mount up with wings like eagles,
> They shall run and not be weary,
> They shall walk and not faint (NKJV, emphasis added).

How much more power could one receive than the strength to mount up, run, walk, and not faint?

How does prayer in your life and church compare to prayer that brings revival, action, power, miracles, and excitement?

_____

_____

_____

_____

_____

_____

Torrey encouraged people who said they were weak and powerless to serve God in His supernatural ability, not in their own natural ability. He said,

> The religion of Jesus Christ is a supernatural religion from start to finish, and we should live our lives in supernatural power, the power of God through Jesus Christ, and we should perform our service with supernatural power, the power of God ministered by the Holy Spirit. It is ours to have the power of God, *if we will only seek it by prayer* in any and every line of service to which God calls us.

Through prayer, we will see revival. God's Holy Spirit will bring it. Dramatic healing, mending of broken relationships, and the compulsion to witness are released by God's Holy Spirit living in us when we invite Him through prayer to release His power. God's Spirit makes a way to us through prayer in the darkest hours of our lives. It is prayer—men and women coming together and crying out to God—that brings God's answers and releases God's power.

R. A. Torrey determined to teach people about the power of prayer, saying, "Prayer often avails where everything else fails." When I replay the tape of my life, I can mark the turning points when God's supernatural power was released in my life because of prayer:

- My salvation
- Healing from alcoholism and addiction
- Being called into ministry
- Unbridled desire to evangelize strangers
- The concept and birth of My Partner Ministries (now Change Your Life) and of *My Partner Prayer Notebook*

In chapter 16 of *Let Prayer Change Your Life*, I share that I believe that God's power—in the person of the Holy Spirit—is released in us when we pray. In Acts 1:8, Jesus promised that after He left the earth, He would send the Holy Spirit to empower His disciples, and the Holy Spirit would be their Counselor, Comforter, and Teacher. Paul taught about the Holy Spirit in Ephesians 3:16–17: "I pray that out of his glorious riches he may strengthen you with power through his Spirit in your inner being, so that Christ may dwell in your hearts through faith."

If you are not knowledgeable about the Spirit-filled life, I suggest that you research your Bible and read additional resources about the person and power of the Holy Spirit in the believer's life. (Campus Crusade for Christ, especially, has many materials available. Books you might want to read include *The Holy Spirit* by Billy Graham, *The Wonderful Spirit-*

Filled Life by Charles Stanley, and *The Helper* by Catherine Marshall.)

In my experience, having not been raised in a church setting that explained the Holy Spirit, I found it helpful to read, study, and understand the third person of the Trinity. Because I was not intimidated by or raised with reservations about the Holy Spirit, I was (and remain) very open to the fullness, abundance, and supernatural power of the Holy Spirit in my life. I have only found more of God when I have daily prayed, asking and inviting the Holy Spirit to "fill me up to overflowing with an extra measure." I encourage you to do the same!

CHAPTER 22

Prayer Unleashes Love for God

Back in 1984, I never would have imagined that I would pray for one hour each day. And if I had been asked what I thought would be the greatest result of my prayer hours, I probably would have guessed that there would be more fruit in my ministry and that I would see more conversions to Christ. Before prayer was a priority in my life, my goals were to be a dynamic communicator and a bold evangelist.

Since 1984, neither of these goals has been my greatest personal gain from prayer. Prayer has been unquestionably the single most significant reason that I have grown a heart full of love for the Lord.

When I was a young Christian in 1976, my love for God grew because of how much He changed me, spared me, forgave me, provided for me, and healed me. When I got through those very needy stages, my fervent prayer life faded. In 1984, when I rediscovered prayer as my source of daily power, once again I began to grow in my love for the Lord—and with true feeling and emotion!

Prayer gave my whole life a new outlook.

I no longer saw my ministry position as a "job." Instead, I was renewed in my desire to serve the Lord.

I no longer felt "trapped," having to obey God because I was a Christian. I obeyed Him because I loved Him and wanted to please Him.

I no longer found prayer boring. I anticipated having a personal appointment with the King of kings!

I no longer was comfortable with compromise, inconsistency, or sin. Because of daily prayer, I felt immediate conviction and shame when I sinned.

In fact, as I confess and expose personal sin, I have an emotional response, a feeling that my Father has been hurt and that I, His child, have embarrassed or shamed Him. I notice that my cheeks redden and my heart feels heavy. But when I repent, His tender love restores and reconciles me to Him within moments.

Once, when my son made an obedience mistake in his relationship with God, I felt the strong emotions of a parent whose child had hurt the grandparent—sadness, regret, even physical discomfort in my stomach. I wanted to confess, explain, and address my Father with my son, so that we would *all* quickly experience right relationships with one another.

And it is the strong emotion of love that also prompts me to respond to God's creation as a gift to us! My natural reaction to a pleasant, serene, sunny day is to whisper, "I love You, Lord," recognizing my Father's intimacy and presence in my life.

Because of daily two-way conversations, I found myself falling in love with the Lord all over again—and I've been falling ever since!

The single most wonderful blessing of prayer in my life has been a deeper love for God that has been unleashed in me.

Should our love relationship with God be considered any different from our other relationships? If we, for whatever reason, neglect to spend time with God, is that love? I have found no better illustration than this excerpt from *The God Who Comes* by Carlo Carretto:

> If a fiancé telephones his fiancée to tell her, "I'm sorry, this evening I can't come, I've so much work!" there is nothing wrong. But if it is the thousandth time he has made the same call, he has not been to see her in weeks on the excuse of work outings with friends, it is more serious—rather, it is quite clear: this is not love. . . .
>
> If you don't pray, if you are not searching for a personal relationship with God, if you don't stay with him for long periods in order to know him, study him, understand him, little by little you will start forgetting him, your memory will weaken, you will no longer recognize him. You will not be able to, because you will no longer know how to love.
> . . . Have you
>   been not praying,
>   not seeking him personally
>   because you don't love him or
>   because you have no time?

How do you respond to this excerpt?

_____

_____

_____

_____

_____

_____

_____

_____

_____

As you've come to this point in *Let Prayer Change Your Life Workbook*, I encourage you not to consider this the end of the book but the *beginning* of your prayer adventure!

Of all the things I do, write, speak about, and enjoy, I feel most used of God and in the midst of His will when I call or challenge people to a prayer commitment. In fact, it is during those times that I most sense God's Holy Spirit within me, directing me.

I encourage you to consider making a decision—or commitment—to spend time with the Lord on a daily basis. Though Scripture doesn't dictate a certain amount of time or demand which part of the day to spend in prayer, the Bible does illustrate over and over that daily prayer is a child of God's privilege, power source, and connection to and with God. I believe that to avoid, eliminate, or overlook this special, personal, intimate time with God would be a person's greatest loss.

Now, I'm not saying that you won't struggle with the (occasional) inconvenience of prayer or with the perseverance it takes to hold on until you receive an answer to prayer. I'm not guaranteeing that you will see immediate answers to prayer, but not one person has yet to tell me differently! In fact, most people start their letters to me with, "You won't believe how my life has changed because of daily prayer!" Nor am I promising that you will become a morning person, *loving* to crack the dawn and pray! What I am suggesting is, "Do it. Just do it!" Take the plunge. Make the time for prayer in your life.

Before you turn the page to the last chapter, called "The Commitment," take a few minutes to reflect on my challenge, and then move forward with a willing and expectant heart!

CHAPTER 23

THE COMMITMENT

At the end of every prayer workshop, I remind each person that I believe all Christians can be powerful and effective pray-ers if they will do these things:

Discover prayer as a conversation,

decide to pray for a certain amount of time each day, and have a

design for prayer that includes My P.A.R.T. in

*P*raise
*A*dmit
*R*equest and
*T*hank-You prayers,

and God's PART in

*L*istening
*M*essages
*N*ew Testament
*O*ld Testament and
*P*roverbs.

At this time, I encourage you to take these steps toward a powerful and effective prayer life by writing out your intentions.

At this time in my life, _____ (date), I,
_____, have ☐ discovered or
☐ rediscovered prayer (check one) to be a powerful two-way conversation between me and the Lord.

I make a decision to spend _____ (fill in a certain amount of time, no less than ten minutes) every day in an appointment with the King, talking to Him as well as listening to Him.

I realize that if I plan ahead for this appointment, I will better avoid interruptions and be able to experience the excitement and intimacy of a two-way conversation with God. Therefore, whenever possible, my usual meeting place with God will be _____
_____
and the approximate time of day (or part of day) that will work best for my lifestyle and commitments will be _____
_____
_____
_____.

(Be as specific as you would like to be.)

I have learned many principles and patterns for prayer and am most comfortable with a design for my prayer life that is as follows. (List the tools you will use to enhance your appointment, such as *My Partner Prayer Journal*, a Bible, a spiral note-book, etc. Include your plan for prayer, such as praising, listening, and requesting.)

_____

_____

_____

_____

_____

_____

_____

Until I have found the disciplined prayer life to be a priority in my life, I will ask _____ *(name of a person)* to keep me accountable to my commitment. I asked him or her to be my accountability partner on _____ *(date)* and he or she agreed!

In your own words, surrender your ability to be successful in this decision, ask for God's help, and express your desire and intentions to the Lord to discover prayer, decide to pray, and have a design for prayer.

_____

_____

_____

_____

_____

_____

_____

_____

FASTING: THE NEXT STEP

Fasting reduces the power of self so that the Holy Spirit can do a more intense work within us.
—Dr. Bill Bright,
excerpt from *The Coming Revival*

My hope is that by the time you have come to the final chapter of the *Let Prayer Change Your Life Workbook* and book, you will have truly . . .

- become a person who better understands and enjoys prayer,
- experienced some of the exciting benefits of a consistent prayer life,
- seen God work in ways that cannot be explained outside His help and intervention, and
- developed a hunger for *more of God!*

MORE OF GOD

In May of 1995, ten years after I began to pray one hour a day, I was challenged—to the point of action—by Dr. Bill

Bright of Campus Crusade for Christ to incorporate the spiritual discipline of fasting into my life. At that time, I was not very familiar with fasting. So the first thing I did after hearing him speak was to plunge into reading a variety of books to help me better understand all aspects of fasting.

In a short amount of time, I was compelled to add fasting to my life on a regular basis. Though many areas of my life began to change, it was the emotional place within me that found revelation and healing because of this new discipline. In fact, from my very first fast until now (many years later), I continue to find that fasting is an exercise that takes me to a deeper level of surrender and sacrifice than I experience with prayer alone.

Whether you are familiar with the discipline of fasting or completely unfamiliar with the subject, I would encourage you to consider adding fasting to your prayer life for two reasons:

1. It will bring an increased awareness of God into your life.
2. It will release unseen work, battle, and power on the earth and in heaven!

Give a brief description of your knowledge and/or experience with fasting.

_____

_____

_____

_____

Are you open to incorporating the spiritual discipline of fasting into your life at this time? Why or why not.

_____

_____

_____

_____

WHERE TO BEGIN

Fasting can have a variety of purposes and many exciting results, but at its core, it should have its focus on God and be done with a humbled heart and pure motives.

In addition to the resources on the topic of fasting found in bookstores, stories found in the Bible will give you an historic picture of why people fast and how God responds! For example, in the book of Esther we read that Esther fasted for three days before going to a person in authority with a request that would affect the lives of many. In 2 Chronicles 20, King Jehoshaphat chose to fast before he went into battle with a vast army. The exact details of their experiences before, during, and after their fast can be very instrumental in directing and motivating you through your own fasts.

One of the most practical guides I found to help bring fasting into the twentieth and twenty-first centuries for me was Dr. Bright's book, *The Coming Revival: A Call to Fasting and Prayer.*

In addition to describing what happens when people fast, it gives very practical suggestions on *how* to fast (juice fasts, water only, one-day fasts, etc.) It seems particularly helpful in taking a skeptical person with no experience in fasting and giving him or her both the courage and the desire to partake of a fast—whether it be a small commitment or a more extended fast.

(Note: In addition to the above-mentioned book, the booklet *Seven Basic Steps to Fasting*, and almost every other book that I read on fasting, directs you to consult with a doctor before partaking of any type of fast.)

Do you currently know of any physical reasons that you should not fast? If so, what are some other ways or areas from which you could fast or abstain? (i.e. watching television, eating desserts, talking, etc.)

_____

_____

_____

PREPARING TO FAST

A fast should be preceded by a time of confession, prayer, amends-making, and Bible reading. Why? Because you are about to engage in a battle with your mind, body, and spirit. At any given moment during a fast, you might experience

- an intense affection for food,
- a struggle with your true motives and purpose for fasting, and

- an awareness of the varying degrees of discipline you exhibit in this area of your life in comparison to other areas your life.

If you are aware of the above issues before a fast, you will not be caught off guard if they arise during your fast. Instead, your spirit should be prepared in advance to exhibit control over your mind and body, reminding the warring parts of yourself that you have a powerful and noble reason for fasting!

Arthur Wallis said, "Fasting is calculated to bring a note of urgency and persistence into our praying, and to give force to our pleas in the court of heaven."

Before you start a fast, rather than be defeated because of a mental or physical weakness, engage in many honest conversations with God about your desire and determination to fast. I encourage you to discuss the specific details of your fast with God: the length of time you plan to fast and your defined purpose(s).

This "preconference" should be a time of reflection and confession during which you ask God to bring to mind any areas or issues that need to be resolved, healed, and cleansed. (I often feel an urge to make amends with certain people during this time.)

I have become convinced that *before* I can begin to fast with power and focus, I must make a number of specific "food" decisions, resolve any unresolved issues (if possible), and "clean house"!

This spiritual and emotional preparation allows me to stay passionate and purposeful during a fast, while at the same time I remain firm in my resolve not to eat even when I feel hungry.

Do any unresolved issues, areas of unforgiveness, or out-of-control patterns come to your mind as you read the preceding paragraphs? Briefly share these thoughts.

_____

_____

_____

Would you be willing to journal about the above thoughts in the next twenty-four hours? If so, set a specific time on your calendar to do this; if you are not willing to do this, to the best of your ability, express your reservations.

_____

_____

Deciding to Fast

Shortly after reading Dr. Bright's book, I followed his suggestion to *lay out a specific plan* for my first fast. After much thought and prayer, I decided to partake of a forty-day *partial* fast, rather than to attempt a *complete* fast. (Note: A complete fast would mean drinking only water and abstaining from all food products, including juices. A partial fast includes abstinence from certain foods or all foods, but not from liquid juices or broths.)

For my first forty-day "partial" fast, I determined to fast from all food for ten days, drinking only juices. The next twenty days I would drink juices until dinnertime, then have a dinner of fruit and vegetables only. The remaining ten days of my fast included three meals of fruit, vegetables, and grains.

Take a look at your month-at-a-glance and/or a twelve-month calendar. Choose the least busy or least stressful time of your family and work life; these are the best times for fasting. For example, plan your fast over a quiet weekend when the kids are away, when you do not have house guests, or when your work situation is not in "high" season of productivity or deadline.

Is there a time in the next few weeks or months that you could fast for one meal or for twenty-four hours?

_____

What time of day would your fast begin? (Ex.: from morning until morning, or from evening to evening)

_____

Record your scheduled fast onto your calendar as you would any other important appointment or commitment. This will give you a visual reminder not to make other conflicting appointments during that twenty-four-hour period, especially on days that might include sharing or preparing special meals. It is also wise to notify your family members of your fasting schedule, so you don't create unmet expectations or miscommunications over mealtimes during your fast.

Designing a Fast

My first fast followed many of the guidelines found in Dr. Bright's book:

- I limited my exercise during those forty days.
- I chose a forty-day period when I did not have a heavy travel schedule or workload.
- I purchased a juicer, in order to drink nonacidic juices, such as apple or carrot juice, during my days of all-liquid fasting.

Most important, I defined a threefold purpose for fasting. In addition to praying for the spiritual condition of our country, I asked God to show me what part I ought to play in bringing about a reconciliation of individuals, marriages and families *with Him*. And third, I prayed for breakthrough in my own son's life (a teenager at that time). During this period of fasting, my entire prayer time became more intense. I also prayed more diligently for those who had specific and sometimes desperate needs and concerns. (Little did I know, and am only learning after five years of fasting on a regular basis, that no matter what one's planned agenda is for a fast, very shortly into a fast, one's motives and heart become exposed to God—and God becomes the focus of the fast.)

Who or what situation come to your mind when you think of fasting for something special or for a breakthrough?

_____

_____

_____

_____

_____

WHAT SHOULD YOU EXPECT TO HAPPEN WHEN YOU FAST?

Within the first six days of my first fast, I experienced a definite—and very long-awaited—breakthrough. First, a friend whom I had prayed for daily and who had been unemployed for more than a year got a job! Also, midway though the fast, an exciting opportunity opened up for me to expand my work of speaking and writing. And by the end of the fast, my teenage son had found a fun, new group of friends at school. (As I look back now, over six years later, this was a definite turning point in every area of my son's life: socially, emotionally, spiritually, and relationally!)

In addition, at least once a day, my own heart and mind were being broken and humbled to see areas in which *I* needed to change, soften, surrender, and heal.

Just as prayer had transformed every area of my life, the results of my first fast had an impact on every area of my life—physically, emotionally, mentally, and spiritually. I began to see and attribute these breakthroughs to the powerful combination of fasting *and* prayer.

Physically

While abstaining from food, I was surprised to find how important and pleasurable food really was to me. Because I was not eating, I realized how often I wanted to eat simply for emotional comfort, to better enjoy a social gathering, or just to satisfy certain cravings.

Without eating for pleasure or comfort, I became very aware of how dependent I had become on food for emotional satisfaction, rather than as nutritional fuel for my body! I can honestly say that my body and mind affectionately fought over food for forty days! Fortunately, as time went on, I experienced a complete disinterest, even a dislike, for certain foods such as meat, cheese, and sweets, none of which were included in my fast.

(Note: If you are currently on a weight reduction or maintenance routine, it will be important to avoid weighing yourself at any point before, during, or after your fast. Though it is probable that you might lose weight during a fast, most people's bodies will gradually regain the weight that was lost during a fast shortly afterwards. Thus, for those who think that weight loss is a primary benefit of spiritual fasting, it is usually short-lived. And if you are not *very* careful, you can easily overeat when you are off of a fast!)

In your most transparent and honest way (depending upon the confidentiality and safety of your group), share where you are with your desire to fast as it relates to your physical body. (Ex. Is it tempting for you to consider a fast in hope of losing weight? Are you afraid to be hungry? Are you fearful of giving up certain foods? Do you currently struggle with issues related to eating, etc.?)

_____

_____

(Note: Though the discipline of fasting may be an integral part of eventually changing an inappropriate appetite, if you struggle with an eating disorder, the discipline of spiritual fasting might be best limited to areas other than eating, and/or monitored by your doctor and spiritual advisers. Because fasting can be the very tool God uses to break unhealthy appetites of any kind in your life, before a fast be prayerful and accountable to those in leadership over you.)

Emotionally and Spiritually

My first fast was motivating in every sense. I was surprised to discover a reserve of willpower that I didn't know existed within me. Later, I would come to understand that it was probably more of a supernatural power than my own strength giving me courage to abstain from the food that I loved, enjoyed, and missed. *I believe that this was the power of the Holy Spirit overriding my mind and body's desire for food, and helping me to do something that was not easy to do— for benefits that I might only later experience.*

As I am writing this addendum, I am currently fasting for three days. Every few hours, I negotiate with myself about the length of time that I have determined to fast. Sometimes my resolve to proceed continues simply because I have told a few of my closest friends that I am doing this! When I consider the humiliation of telling my friends that I gave up, my wandering thoughts and tempted mind are defeated! But in the spiritual realm, the power that is displayed when calling a group of people to fast and pray for a specific purpose is best modeled by Esther and King Jehoshaphat in the Bible. (see Esther 4:16 2 Chron. 20:3.)

It is important to have a number of deterrents to keep you from giving in or giving up early during a fast:

- Post or mark out the fast on your calendar.
- Ask a few people to either keep you accountable or to join you in a fast.
- Eliminate certain foods from your kitchen during a fast.
- Plan, in advance, when and where you will have a juice break.
- Avoid scheduling a meal appointment during a fast.

Share any other ideas that have worked to keep you strong in your resolve to abstain during a fast.

_____

_____

_____

_____

Upon completing my first partial fast, I sensed I that I was embarking on an exciting spiritual adventure and I wanted to experience more of God! Just as I had been convinced that regular, consistent, planned times of prayer could change my life, I had become convinced that regular fasting was another discipline that could deepen my relationship with God and bring about change in my life, and even the world.

CONTINUING THE DISCIPLINE

In the beginning, fasting seemed overwhelming, but by having a plan, I have been able to fast hundreds of meals for the purpose of seeing breakthrough in my life and the world.

I share these numbers with you to serve as both an encouragement and a true life illustration that even with a busy travel and work schedule, a spouse and child, as well as other commitments, a busy and even undisciplined person *can* incorporate the spiritual discipline of fasting into his life on a regular basis.

As with prayer, I have found the spiritual discipline of fasting has caused me to know God better and has deepened my desire to make Him known.

From the many authors I have researched on the subject of fasting, I have come to some conclusions:

- Fasting is a spiritual discipline that not only Jesus spoke about and modeled (Mark 9:29; Matt. 4:2ff), but also Old Testament figures partook of in order to see breakthrough in their lives and for their countries (e.g., Esther, Daniel, Jehoshaphat, Ezra, Nehemiah, etc.).
- Fasting involves a fresh humbling and submission of oneself unto God with results that are not always expected and do not always remain private!

Especially because of the positive changes I saw in my son's life during my first fast, I concluded that I should continue to fast once a week for him throughout his high school years (sometimes one meal, or from morning until dinner, and most often for twenty-four hours). Even though he is now in his twenties, I still fast once a week for him! What compels me to continue? Because I have observed that during or immediately following times of fasting and prayer for him, we have the most interesting, meaningful, and loving conversations—and occasionally the most powerful of break-throughs will occur.

In your life, name the people, situations, or organizations for whom you feel inclined to fast and pray.

_____

_____

_____

_____

_____

It has now been more than five years since I added the spiritual discipline of fasting to my life. God has called me to two forty-day and two thirty-day partial fasts during that time, as well as many shorter and more spontaneous fasts for special purposes. During those years, I have kept a fasting journal in addition to my prayer journal. And not until mid-way through this experience did it occur to me to add up all of my twenty-four-hour fasts. By October 23, 1998, I completed my nonconsecutive fortieth day of fasting! And because I found the experience to be so important to my spiritual growth and in staying focused on praying for our country, in 1999, I made a decision to fast for our country another forty days before the end of the year 2000. (I have six months to go and am only ten days away from fulfilling that commitment—and it is only June. In all honesty, the second forty days has been harder than the first forty days of fasting. Interestingly, it has often been the fact that I had written of my decision to partake of a second forty-day, nonconsecutive fast in the book, _Let Prayer Change Your Life_ that really kept me going! I am convinced that if I had not written those words for others to see, I would have not have undertaken such an extensive fast! I know myself. I do not like to be hungry! I will not pursue something difficult if it is an idea that is only swirling around in my mind. I need accountability and support. I will give up too easily if others aren't both cheering for me or watching to see if I succeed. Yet, I also know the result of fasting and the breakthrough that it brings and want so much for others to experience the blessings. But, to encourage others to fast or even to call others to join in a fast, one must be able to master the discipline. Thus, I find incredible strength in the accountability as a result of my public and personal pledge to fast for revival in America. And not only have I grown more deeply in love with the Lord, more challenged in all of my relationships to be a kind and more generous person, and clearer in focus to achieve the call I believe God has put in my life, but hundreds of people have begun to fast for breakthrough in their lives and for revival in America!

Now it is time for you to make some decisions regarding fasting!

1. Will you consider fasting and praying for the spiritual health and reconciliation of our country with God?_____

2. Will you gather up all of the resources you can regarding fasting for spiritual breakthrough and read them

with an open heart and mind? If so, when will you purchase or acquire these resources?

_____

3. Will you—in the next seven days—pray about the kind of fast God would have you undertake? Fasting does not always mean abstinence from food; it could include abstaining from television, certain foods, etc.

_____

Fasting is not confined to abstinence from eating and drinking. Fasting really means voluntary abstinence for a time from the various necessities of life, such as food, drink, sleep, rest, association with people and so forth. The purpose . . . is to loosen to some degree the ties which bind us to the world of material things and our surroundings as a whole, in order that we may concentrate all our spiritual powers upon the unseen and eternal things.[1]

4. Are you willing to pray for specific breakthrough for yourself and others? I strongly recommend fasting if you (a) have come to an impasse in a situation, (b) have not been able to overcome a weakness, (c) are desperate for an answer, or (d) need special wisdom in a specific situation

_____

_____

5. Describe any situation, impasse, weaknesses, addic-

tions, or special need for which you would like to specifically fast:

_____

_____

_____

_____

I have found that fasting, if done with a prayerful purpose, over time, *will* result in change and breakthrough. As cautioned in many of the books I read on the spiritual discipline of fasting, a one-meal, one-day, or onetime fast does not guarantee that a change will occur in a situation any more than a one-minute prayer might be considered an effective way to bring about a significant change.

If you decide to fast, take time to prepare:

Detail a fasting plan on your calendar. If you schedule your fasting times—in writing—in advance, you will be more likely to follow through with the plan, rather than being caught off guard by unexpected appointments or forgetfulness.

Define your purpose for fasting in a fasting and prayer journal. Make these purposes the focus of your prayer time during the fast. Write them down in a journal and record and date any breakthroughs or changes. These journal entries will give you motivation to proceed when your endurance levels get low.

Prepare yourself physically. Consult a doctor before beginning a partial or complete fast. Expect that your energy levels will be lower than normal, therefore do not maintain a rigorous exercise schedule during a fast. A daily walking plan might be the best way to increase your energy level without exhausting yourself physically.

Prepare yourself emotionally and spiritually. A time of transparent, honest confession (to God and to others) prior to any fast is essential for having a clean and ready heart, mind, and spirit. Unforgiveness, unresolved issues, or unconfessed sin will hinder answered prayer and any breakthrough that would otherwise result from fasting.

Be accountable to another person. It is often easier to fast when others know that you are fasting or especially when they are fasting along with you.

Expect breakthrough and *opposition.* Whenever a believer desires to grow, change, seek more of God, or attempt to do something great for God, there will be discouraging setbacks and incredible interventions. Daily time spent reading and studying the Word of God will result in increased faith and endurance during the "up and down" times that occur during every fast. You will be given courage and strength to sustain you during a fast as you uncover in God's Word how others persevered, attempted great things, and believed what they could not see.

ARE YOU INTERESTED?

I used to think that prayer was boring and that fasting was for monks. Since discovering the power of fasting *combined* with prayer, I've determined to make these two disciplines a regular part of my life. I am now personally convinced that fasting, in addition to prayer, *increases*

- a listening and sensitive spirit.
- a humbled heart and attitude.
- a willingness to make temporary sacrifices for a more permanent cause or outcome.
- an extra measure of inner discipline that prompts increased outer discipline.
- awareness of an unseen world where spiritual powers are at war.
- an eagerness and urgency that does not wane in the waiting.
- a determination that is sustained.
- a willingness to follow through on steps of obedience, even though they may be uncomfortable or uneasy.

Share any intentions, reservations, thoughts, plans, or purposes that you have at this time about the spiritual discipline of fasting.

_____

_____

_____

If you are motivated to the point of developing a fasting plan, please describe yours:

_____

_____

Can you think of anything hindering you from fasting? (Ex.: improper attitude, unconfessed sin, impure motive, fear of failure or of hunger, etc.)

_____

_____

Consider a time of meditation and prayer before laying out or beginning to fast. Would you be willing to place that time of prayer on your calendar now or give yourself one month to read more about fasting? If so, when will you do this, and if not, why not?

_____

_____

_____

It is my sincere hope that you will want to learn more about fasting by asking *God* what He would have you to do with this spiritual discipline. If your deepest desire is know God better, I believe that fasting will increase your awareness of God's voice, touch, and presence—every time you fast!

Be encouraged,
Becky

Be encouraged! Your decision to make prayer a priority in your life is not meant to be legalistic or restricting. It is meant to help you develop the discipline it takes to draw near to the Lord, pour your heart out to Him, and find forgiveness and experience healing through daily conversations with the King.

If you fall short, forget to pray, or encounter old pitfalls, don't be defeated or get bogged down with guilt. Instead, pick up where you left off and start over. God is not interested in making you feel guilty for missing your time with Him! He just wants to be with you! Spend time with Him and . . .

Let prayer change your life!

Sincerely in Christ,

Becky Tirabassi

If you are interested in obtaining any of Becky Tirabassi's materials—such as *My Partner Prayer Journal*, books, videos, or audios—or would like information on how to sponsor or attend a Let Prayer Change Your Life workshop, please contact by letter, phone, or fax:

Becky Tirabassi Change Your Life®, Inc.
Box 9672
Newport Beach, CA 92660
1-800-444-6189 (phone)
949-644-8044 (fax)
www.changeyourlifedaily.com

ORDER FORM

Qty	Item	ISBN	Cost Each	Total
	Let Prayer Change Your Life	0-7852-6885-5	10.99	
	My Partner Prayer Journal	0-7852-6382-9	16.99	
	Refills for My Partner Prayer Journal	0-7852-7482-0	10.99	
	Change Your Life Daily Bible	0-8423-3289-8	20.00	
	Let Prayer Change Your Life Workbook	0-7852-6658-5	19.00	
	Let Faith Change Your Life	0-7852-7235-6	17.99	
	Let Love Change Your Life	0-7852-6509-0	14.99	
			Subtotal	
	California residents add 7.75% sales tax			
			Subtotal	
	Add $2.50 postage for each product ordered			
	Handling Charge			
			TOTAL	

Name

Address

City   State   Zip

Telephone   E-mail

❑ Visa   ❑ MC   ❑ Discover   ❑ American Express

Account # _____ Exp. Date:_____

These items may be purchased at most bookstores or send this form, along with credit card information or a check or money order for the total amount, to:

Becky Tirabassi Change Your Life, Inc.®
Box 9672
Newport Beach, CA 92660
Fax: 1-949-644-8044
Phone: 1-800-444-6189
www.changeyourlifedaily.com

NOTES

NOTES

NOTES

NOTES

NOTES

NOTES

NOTES

NOTES